STEAMING *through* BRITAIN

STEAMING *through* BRITAIN

MILES KINGTON

PHOTOGRAPHY BY

ALAIN LE GARSMEUR

UNWIN

HYMAN

LONDON SYDNEY WELLINGTON

First published in Great Britain by the Trade Division of Unwin Hyman Limited, 1990.

UNWIN HYMAN LIMITED
15-17 Broadwick Street
London W1V 1FP

Allen & Unwin Australia Pty Ltd
8 Napier Street, North Sydney, NSW
2060, Australia

Allen & Unwin New Zealand Pty Ltd
with the Port Nicholson Press
Compusales Building, 75 Ghuznee
Street, Wellington, New Zealand

British Library Cataloguing in Publication Data
Kington, Miles, *1941–*
Steaming through Britain.
1. Great Britain. Steam railway services –
Illustrations
I. Title II. Le Garsmeur, Alain
385'.5'0941

ISBN 0-04-440488-3

Designed by Julian Holland

Printed in Hong Kong by:

Sing Cheong Printing Co. Ltd.

Contents

Introduction

MOST TRAIN books are written by people who know a lot about railways. This one is a little different. A lot of knowledge can be a dangerous thing – dangerously informative, dangerously ponderous and dangerously boring. Often I have leapt up from the perusal of a railway book and cried: 'If only this chap knew less and told me more!'

There is, for instance, a bloke called Wilson (he admits to no first name) who puts out every year a complete timetable of all the private steam lines in Britain, scores of them, and gets the times as near right as is possible. He also adds his own comments and description to each line, and this must be what prompts him to say at the beginning that if anyone is offended by his opinions, then they are welcome to their own. The way he defends his opinions you might think he had made fearless criticisms of some lines, but there is not one single adverse remark to be found anywhere in the entire book. Not one. He is under the illusion that he is being outspoken, but he is merely coy. It's all detail, no colour.

This is true of all writing on steam lines. Packed with facts, but not much wider view. So rather than compete with the learned boys, I thought it would be fun to write nine essays on Britain's top steam runs, not to tell you which engines can be found where (if you want to know that, it's 100-1 you know already), but to give some idea of why one line is different from another *in character*. Why lines feel different from each other, in fact, rather than how long they are. So I didn't do any rooting around in reference books; instead, I rode up and down on the trains, talked to lots of people and tried to get the pulse of a place. Some lines I liked better than others and if that doesn't come out in the book as you go along, then it's not the book I set out to write.

Alain le Garsmeur has journeyed in the same direction with his photographs. They are not the sort of photograph under which you can write, as rail books normally do, 'A British Rail-built Class 5 working a load of 1938 Swindon-built trucks up the 1-in-80 incline near etc. etc.' Most of the photographs don't really need captions at all – they convey the atmosphere of the lines in a way which sometimes makes a writer despair. Mark you, we were taken in quite different directions – I stuck close to where people were, and he took a bird's eye view, so our paths rarely crossed, but every now and then I would spot a glint of light up on a hillside and think to myself: Le Garsmeur at work!

Our choice of lines will strike some readers as pretty conventional, but we felt we had to go for the best, and the most developed. These things change over the years. Two or three years back I received a letter from my birthplace in Northern Ireland, Downpatrick, saying that they were thinking of reviving the old Downpatrick to Ardglass Railway and would I chuck in a couple of bob? I splashed out on a life membership and now, in 1990, the Railway already has locos running, a station, rolling stock, track. ... From acorn to small oak in such a short time. Who knows how far it will go? In fact, it would be tempting to do a book on the odd steam lines of Britain – the one on the Isle of Mull, the one made entirely by a clergyman in Leicestershire, the one owned by the Chairman of ScotRail... and the Downpatrick one, of course.

But this is our report on the best of British steam today, in which we've tried to give a flavour guide to each one. Somewhere in the book I've suggested that steam lines age and mature like wines, and sometimes go over the top, and maybe there should be a way of describing the way they taste too. If this book gives you a notion to go out and taste for yourself, or gets you comparing experiences, then that's a good start.

Right: *LMS Stanier class 5 No. 5407 racing along the side of Mallerstang Valley on the Settle to Carlisle line.*

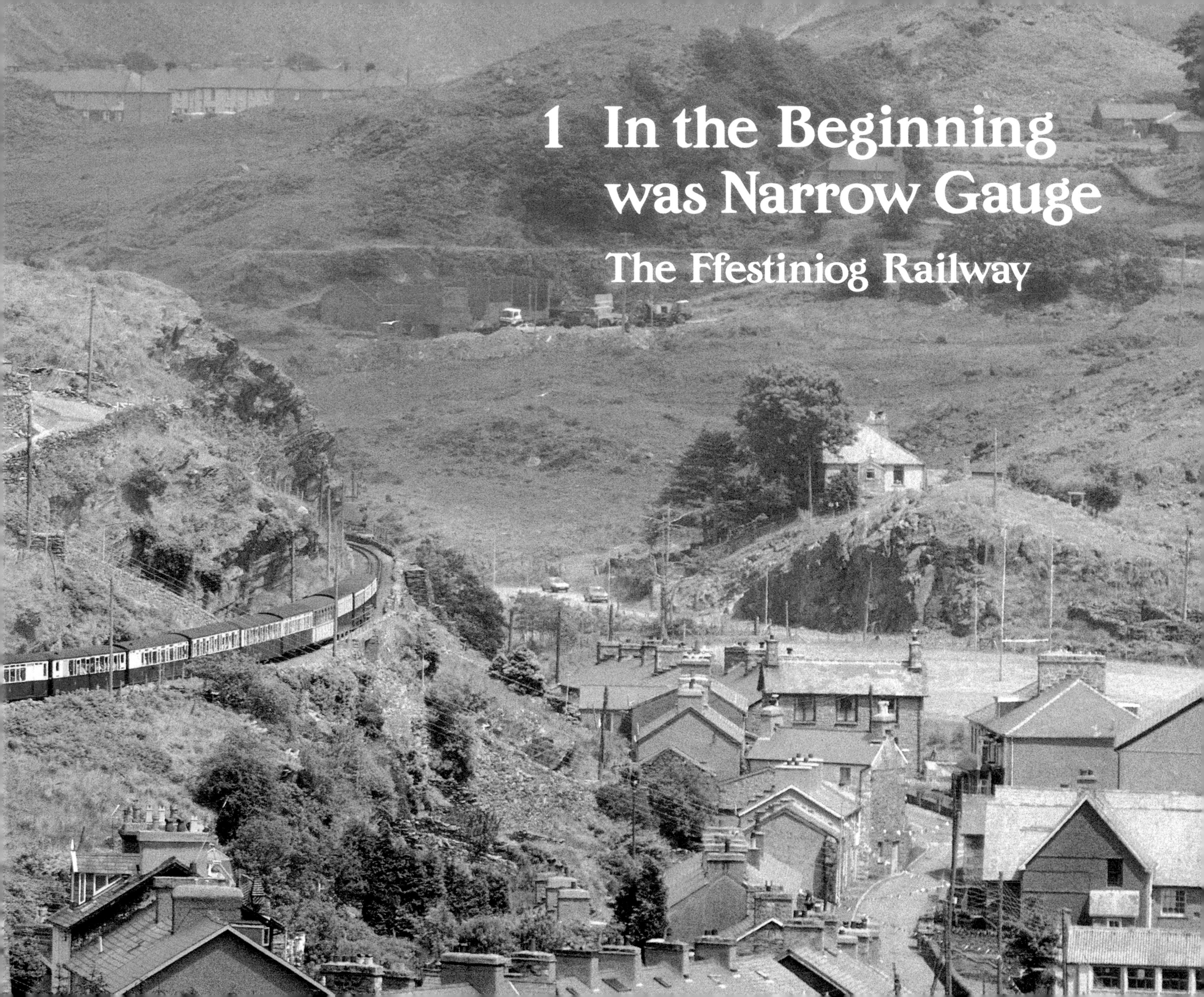

1 In the Beginning was Narrow Gauge

The Ffestiniog Railway

THIS MAY sound strange, but the Festiniog Railway reminds me very much of a photographic museum I once visited on the island of Madeira. It was more than a museum, it was a working studio which had been in the same family ever since it was founded in the 1840s, the birthday years of photography. Now, Madeira is a long way from Portugal, the mother country, and ordering valuable cameras across the stormy seas was a risky business, so the founding father decided to learn how to make his own, and cut out Lisbon altogether. Painstakingly, he built large, shining, varnished wood cameras. He painted enormous backdrops for studio portraits. His son carried on the work and built more cameras, more equipment. Today, they use modern cameras, but they also have all the old equipment, which still works, and sometimes the current old man of the family gets it all out for the day and takes wonderfully clear photos with it, and if you really wanted to have a family portrait done now against one of the 1890s backgrounds (all still carefully stacked in the studio), why, I expect they would do that too.

Well, Portmadoc isn't so far from London as Madeira from Lisbon, and you don't have to cross stormy seas to get there, but back in 1800 London seemed a long way, and in fact the sea journey was the best way of getting there. What they had in the hills above Portmadoc, or below Snowdon, was slate, which was then hugely in demand, and what they wanted was a way of getting the slate down from the hills to the ships which would take it away. A railway, of course. But there was something a bit Madeiran in the way it all came together. First, an embankment was built across the mouth of the River Glaslyn by William Madocks (after whom Portmadoc is named), a local landowner who nearly went bankrupt in the process. Next, it was found that the water pent up by the embankment was scouring out a large, ready-made harbour, and finally a company emerged from all the rivals to start building a railway line in 1833 and who finished it in 1836.

If you read the original Act of Parliament of 1832 which authorised the line, you will find plenty of details about the weight of track, number of trucks etc., but you won't find anything about motive power. Steam engines are not mentioned. This was just as well, because steam engines were not used. In the Madeiran tradition of using the best available solution, the company pulled the trucks to and fro with horses. Even that is not quite true, because they only pulled the empty trucks up with horses (the trip took about eight hours). On the way down the job was done by gravity, and the horses rode for free in so-called dandy cars at the back, while brakemen danced across the top of the trucks, applying and releasing brakes as necessary (the return trip took two hours).

But after twenty or thirty years it became apparent that the heavier loads needed something a bit heavier than horses, and this is where the line became truly Madeiran. Seeing that there was no precedent for steam engines on a narrow, two-foot wide line, the company commissioned special engines to be built and Robert Fairlie designed the engine named after him: the Double Fairlie. At first sight it looks extremely silly, and so it does at second sight: two little steam engines back to back, like Siamese twins, with two independent fireboxes and chimneys, sharing only a boiler and a cab. But the double power made it extremely strong and smooth; you were facing forward whichever way you went, which was a great blessing both for the driver and, in later years, photographers. The whole thing was mounted on bogies so that it could go round the narrowest of corners – in fact, the Festiniog also introduced bogie iron-frame coaches before anyone else did.

In 1870, when the line went over to this new engine, it caused quite a sensation, because nobody had ever expected narrow gauge railways to catch on, let alone lead the way in anything, and for a while small railways all over the world were built in imitation of the Festiniog. The Festiniog Railway became a top tourist attraction, and even before 1900, when tourism is commonly thought of as having been in its infancy, they were already attracting 100,000 passengers a year

Previous page: *The double-header train of* 'Prince' *and* 'Mountaineer' *cutting through the hills to Tanygrisiau station.*

Right: 'Mountaineer' *leaves Blaenau Ffestiniog as it passes through the slate miners' cottages of Penlan.*

101
MOUNTAINEER

Above: 'Merddin Emrys', *a Fairlie double bogie loco built in 1879, prepares to draw out of Portmadoc station.*

Opposite: 'Mountain Prince' *crosses Portmadoc Bay on the Cob as it leaves Portmadoc behind.*

and running eight trains a day, which is pretty wonderful even by modern standards. In those days it was unbelievable.

It becomes sickening after a while just to list all the ways in which the Festiniog Railway did things first, especially if you are from some other railway, but there is no way round it. There is a book by M.J.T. Lewis called *'How Festiniog Got its Railway'*, which takes the story of the line up to the opening in 1836 and then stops. A history of a line which *stops* in 1836! No other line in this book had even thought of *starting* by then, except the NYMR. It's a bit like finding a book called *'How Madeira Got its Photographic Industry'* which comes to an end in 1850.

And it justifies throwing this dollop of history at you. I don't believe, on the whole, that history always helps you enjoy a train journey more. It's interesting to know, as you hurtle from London to Bristol on a 125 that Brunel once cursed the coffee at Swindon station or that nervous travellers were allowed to get out at Box tunnel and take a horse and carriage onwards, but it's not half so interesting as looking out of the window. I think you could safely travel on the Bluebell, or Keighley, or Severn Valley lines, and leave all your history at home without noticing the difference except a lighter tread. But the years behind the Festiniog Railway are so interesting, and there are so many of them, that it does add a different dimension.

For instance, the FR has no less than three interchanges with British Rail. It's enough to make the West Somerset weep, as they look down the blank gap between them and Taunton. The Bluebell Line doesn't go anywhere, either end; what wouldn't they give for a sniff of BR? But the Festiniog is so well equipped with British Rail station interchanges that one of them, at Minffordd, seems to be almost forgotten about. The other two are at Portmadoc and at Blaenau Ffestiniog, at the bottom and the top, and if you look at a map of North Wales you will see that although you can't get round the country by rail if you stick to BR, you *can* plug the missing gap with the Festiniog line. Up the Welsh coast from Aberystwyth to Portmadoc, over to the narrow gauge line, up into the hills, off at Blaenau and change to BR's Conway Valley line which starts there and plunges deep in a slate tunnel to re-emerge heading up to the north coast of Wales. It would take some time, and it's a good walk across Portmadoc from one station to the other, and the Festiniog doesn't run *every* day in winter, but there it is all the same.

The picture I have painted there is of the FR filling in a gap in the BR system, but – and this is where history puts things in quite different focus again – the Festiniog line was there long before the other two. The standard gauge lines were Johnny-comes-latelys by comparison. To look down on British Rail as recently arrived amateurs does give the trip a certain perspective, not to say flavour.

Added flavour is something the trip doesn't really need. The scenery is so grand, and the change of surrounding from harbourside at one end to bleak

mountainside at the other, so melodramatic, that the Festiniog line can afford to turn its nose up at added colourings and flavourings. In fact, it throws away one of its grandest effects right at the start. The train emerges from the Harbour station straight onto the embankment built by Madocks in 1811 – always known as the Cob – and the minute or two it takes to run across it is simply not enough to take in both the landward view, which is a panorama of Snowdonia above a wide estuary, and the seaward view, a glittering expanse of water bounded by promontories, full of herons, cormorants, oyster-catchers and the occasional yacht. Sometimes, in a West End play, the scenery is so well designed that the audience gives it an ovation, much to the fury of the actors. Well, in the first few yards of the Festiniog line, you feel like leaping to your feet and whistling.

Perhaps, in a way, it's like an opera overture in which the composer lets you glimpse all the themes and best bits which you're going to get more of later – in those few seconds the Festiniog scenery throws at you a glorious jumble of mountains, water, sky, rocks and steaming engines, all of which get repeated in a more dignified fashion in the hour's journey to the top. After the excitement of the Cob, and a glimpse on the right of the Boston Lodge engine works, the line becomes almost suburban for a while, working through little villages, behind fields and up the back of Penrhyndeudreath, but beyond that the ascent of the line is a geography lesson...

Right: 'Mountain Prince' *leaves Blaenau Ffestiniog through the houses of Barlwyd Terrace.*

Below: 'Merddin Emrys' *on the Dduallt Spiral, the only rail spiral in Great Britain, as it makes its way to Blaenau Ffestiniog.*

MOUNTAIN
PRINCE

13′-6″

Q *What happens when you go up from the coast in North Wales? Yes, you, boy.*
A *Sir, you leave the valley behind and go up the hill, you get into the trees, then you go above the tree line and get into the bracken, and then after a while you get above that, and it's only grass, sheep and slate.*
Q *Very good. And what's that great lump over to the south?*
A *That's Trawsfynydd Power Station, sir.*
Q *But we don't tell American tourists that, do we. What do we tell them it is?*
A *Harlech Castle, sir.*
Q *And do they believe us?*
A *Quite often, sir.*

The rise is gradual, consistent and never-ending. It had to be, so that it didn't defeat horses on the way up or gravity on the way down, and the twists in the line are explained by the fact that it was more important to keep a gentle gradient than go in a straight line. But the most famous twist of all was caused by something quite different: water. More precisely by the wicked action of the Central Electricity Generating Board in covering the top of the line with a lake at a time when the Festiniog Line never looked like getting back to Blaenau Festiniog. The Festiniog rail people were furious and sued the CEGB for all they could get, but it didn't bring the line back, so in the 1960s they buckled down to build a new line, which involved a complete spiral, a new tunnel and a fresh line along the lake. It was known by the unappealing name of the Deviation but the volunteers who worked on it were proud to be known as Deviationists, and although, by the standards of motorway construction, it was no great shakes, as a purely voluntary effort it is quite staggering.

'Funny thing was,' said Phil, 'that they were only interested in building the Deviation. They kept quite separate from the rest of us. I don't believe they were actually interested in the rest of the railway, or trains, at all. When it was all finished, they all vanished.'

Phil Dowse is a driver, a volunteer. In private life he is also a train driver, out of Paddington, for which he gets paid. He gave me the only footplate ride I got in 1989 (apart from one on the North Yorkshire Moors), so thanks, Phil. When he comes to the Festiniog to do some driving, he finds it hard not to go at 60 mph the first day (there's a 20 mph limit on the line) and finds the rolling stock pretty small. When he gets back to Paddington, it all seems pretty huge and fast, though it would upset the system if he kept to 20 mph on the main line, so he doesn't. Doesn't he get fed up with driving ever?

'I'm taking a few days off on Wednesday, actually. I'm getting the train across to Crewe, then catching one up the West Coast and going to Fort William via Glasgow, then over to Mallaig and on a boat to Skye. Back from there to Lochalsh and over to Inverness, and all the way down again and hopefully get here by Sunday lunchtime to start driving again. Well, it's a break.'

And that's what drivers do in their time off. Mark you, he wasn't always a driver here, and when you go past Dduallt station he sighs with nostalgia at the

Opposite: *Leaving Tan-y-Bwlch,* 'Merddin Emrys' *crosses the cast iron skew bridge with its gothic balustrades.*

Below: 'Merddin Emrys' *approaching Tan-y-Bwlch.*

sight of the now derelict signal box, where he had spent many happy hours in solitary suspension. Actually, being a driver is hardly less solitary; the one thing I have learnt from rare forays to the footplate is that being a driver may bring you closer to the engine, but what it chiefly does is take you further from people. A driver can quite happily forget that the coaches behind him contain passengers, all of whom have paid good money to be on the train and half of whom are coming round to goggle at his engine at the end of the trip. This is the point when he has to go public, like a hermit in a grotto who has suddenly been visited by a coachload of pilgrims.

'Do we have requests for any of the request stops?' Phil asks Nick Corley, the fireman.

'All of them.'

Phil groans.

'Not going to get a good run at the line this time, then.'

All that stopping and starting may be good for passengers but it's a bind for the crew. I like it, because it gives me a chance to catch up with my notes at stations; you can write when the engine's going along all right, but you can't read it afterwards. I have a note here that reads MAD DOG. What can that mean? Oh yes, I remember...

'There's a mad dog on the line,' says Phil. 'He lives somewhere in the woods. There's all kinds of wildlife round here, but he's the wildest.'

And sure enough a black dog appeared on the line in the woods, ranting and raving at the engine and only just getting out of the way in time. That's harder than it sounds. The Festiniog is built with less clearance than any line I've ever seen, on either side, and if you poke your head out in the cuttings you'll knock your false eyelashes off. Up in the woods there are cuttings so tight that there are signs in Welsh and English saying to the rambler the equivalent of 'For God's sake don't walk down here, because there won't be room for both you and a train. If a train comes, the train will win.'

After my footplate ride on the North Yorkshire Moors I had grit in my hair like black dandruff for three days afterwards. Riding on *Linda* on the Festiniog it struck me suddenly as very peculiar that I had no smuts at all, until I remembered the other very Madeiran thing about the line; all the engines have been converted from coal to oil. There was a time in the 1970s when fire danger seemed so great and timber was getting so dear, that they simply felt they had to switch to oil, which creates virtually no sparks at all. Except among the coal-loving community.

'They can't get over it,' says Phil. 'They come and look at the engine for a long time and finally say, 'What's that?' I tell them it's the oil tank. Another long pause and they say, 'Where does the coal go, then?''

Which obviously gives Phil a lot of pleasure. Actually, I was a bit disturbed at first to realise that coal had been phased out altogether, but then you realise that it's merely by custom we associate coal with steam. You could heat it with gas, wood or electricity; what's important is the steam, and in fact oil-firing seems to be easier, more powerful and certainly cleaner. All right, so you miss the steady shovelling of the fireman and all the little rituals of placing one shovelfull *here* and one in *this* corner, but on the other hand you don't set fire to the countryside. 1989 was a long hot summer and most railway lines were plagued with fires. On the Festiniog they didn't phone the fire brigade once.

Other unique things about the line:

1 All preserved lines have religious posters, but only the Festiniog has permanently painted ones, endowed by a local chapel.
2 It is the only one with funny ads in the carriages, done by Browsers Bookshop of Portmadoc.
3 It was never owned by British Rail.
4 It's the only line I came across with a class structure – First, Third and Observation. Observation coaches are so-called because they have plush red armchairs with big wings which prevent you seeing out of the windows.
5 Nobody knows how to spell the name properly.

This last is a more serious point than you might think. You may have noticed that if Ffestiniog is a

Right: *Out of Tan-y-Bwlch station,* 'Merddin Emrys' *hugs Tyler's Curve.*

THIRD
THIRD
THIRD
THIRD
THIRD
22

place-name, it has two 'F's.' If it's the railway, it has one. The Act of Parliament says so, and that should be an end to it. But the railway cannot quite bring itself to believe the Act, and spells it both ways as if uneasily aware that the Parliamentary spelling is an English bastardisation of the correct Welsh spelling – indeed, if you wanted to be pedantic about this, Festiniog with one 'F' should correctly be pronounced Vestiniog.

The reason all this is a bit serious is that the Festiniog Railway has always been perceived, more or less, as an English imposition on Welsh culture. When the CEGB flooded the line near Blaenau Ffestiniog , the locals tended to back the CEGB (who were providing jobs), rather than the line (which was thought to be an English plot to screw the CEGB for some compensation). Very few of the volunteers today, or the owners in the old days, were Welsh, which wouldn't matter so much except that as Welsh identity becomes sharper these days it may be seen as even more of an English invasion.

'They don't like us very much up at Blaenau, you know,' a volunteer muttered to me. So I went to Blaenau to have a look round and I don't think they liked the look of me very much either. It's a cruelly grey town, linked to the slate workings which hang over it, and now caught up in the death of those slate workings; the most prosperous firm I saw was Richard Lewis, the monumental stonemason next to the town cemetery, with a bunch of freshly commissioned stones outside his door, all in Welsh. I went into the second-hand bookshop, Siop Lyfrau'r Hen Bost, and all the time I was in there, half a dozen people came in but not one spoke English. There were many books in Welsh, including Roald Dahl's latest, *The Hungry Crocodile,* and many in English, but not one as far as I could see on the railway. When I paid for two books by cheque, the lady didn't tell me who to make it payable to but silently held out her card for me to copy Siop Lyfrau'r Hen Bost, even though it only means The Old Post Office Book Shop.

It was all quite nostalgic, actually. I grew up in Wrexham, North Wales, where as an English lad I was regularly made to feel a foreigner and a bit unwanted. We had an old gardener called Isaac who had served in a Welsh regiment in the First World War and had been the only man in his unit who could speak *any* English at all. He had to translate all the letters home from the others, so that the officer could censor them. In that context I think I too would feel leery of the English, and indeed I did try to teach myself Welsh back in Wrexham, but all I could find was a Bible in Welsh, which didn't quite work. Nowadays, as I saw at the Siop Lyfrau'r Hen Bost, they have brightly coloured cartoon books and reader-friendly guides to the first steps in Welsh. I think I may have another go soon.

The workforce and the volunteers of the line are almost all English, and I got the feeling that being among the Welsh drew them together. I also got a fainter, but definite, impression that some of them were there precisely because it was far away and, almost, abroad. Rob, for instance, is a trainee driver who should be qualified to drive by 1990 and who, before all this, had a well-paid London job with the John Lewis Partnership. He gave it up to get away from London and the big city, came to North Wales without knowing there were trains up here and is now hooked. He's taken a big cut in income and is much happier than he was, yet I feel he's got satisfaction here which he wouldn't have got, say, by moving to the Bluebell Line.

Andy came up to the Festiniog Line for the 1989 summer season as a fireman. He had been an estate agent in Wimbledon and hated it. When his fireman job ran out, there was a gap as a guard, and he took it in order, really, to avoid a decision about his future. When I last saw him in late September he had already had a five-month summer, the leaves were beginning to turn and he couldn't go on being a guard much longer, unless he opted to go full-time on the line. When you gather with the others in the warmth of the Australia Arms in Portmadoc (currently the preferred railway workers' pub), it must seem the only place in the world to be. When you walk home alone at night

Above: *There's a strong Methodist influence on the line.*

Opposite: 'Mountaineer' *following the Afon Barlwyd into Blaenau Ffestiniog.*

under a remote Welsh sky, with Welsh rain coming down out of it, you must have doubts. I wonder which way he went.

Jo Clulow seems to have no doubts. He is well settled in Portmadoc, with none of the more romantic hankerings of Rob and Andy, and it was his self-appointed task, poor chap, to take me round the Boston Lodge engine works for a technical tour. Never was so much knowledge wasted on such an untechnical mind. But even to me a picture began to emerge of a line which has progress well within its grasp and is unable to take hold of it. So much is being built – coaches, new push-and-pull stock, even new engines – and yet so much crops up that halts progress, such as inability to find the right people, or the right money, or the right work team. As soon as smooth progress is made on something, something else crops up – it may be nothing more than being one driver short, but then someone has to go from the engine shed to take over and his job languishes for another day.

Money? The company can't afford to buy the best oil for the engine fuel, so they get second-hand industrial oil which is put through a centrifuge by Jo to clean out the gunge.

People? Harold Parkes is a super machinist. Unfortunately, he's seventy and will have to retire one day, with no replacement in sight.

Equipment? In good shape, except that every engine wears out sooner or later. *Merddyn Emrys* seems to have a crack in the boiler. *Blanche* is coming in this year for a total refit after eighteen years – 'What they call a jack-up-the-whistle-and-put-a-new-engine-underneath job,' says Jo.

He sounds miserable. He looks anything but. This is all part of the life, grumbling, and bemoaning lacks, and worrying about the bulge in the hillside near the top of the line, and wishing there was more money. When winter comes, and Rob is not on the trains but out helping to mend the permanent way, will he wish he was back with old John Lewis and his partnership? Not on your nelly.

Above: *A volunteers' hostel.*

To a foreign eye like mine, Boston Lodge seems littered with useless, rusting old parts – wheels, axle boxes, unidentifiable bits and bobs. Jo is quite shocked by my ignorance. All these things will come in useful one day, and the rust is, if anything, helping to preserve them, acting as a defensive outer layer, perhaps like snow on a bed of snowdrops. He tells me the instructive tale of the Isle of Man Railway (which he is very sorry to hear is not being featured in this book) and how it was taken over in the 1970s by a man who had run a *bus* company. Well, he bloody well treated the Isle of Man Railway like another bus line, scrapping unused coaches, cutting up old boilers for scrap – you can't do that on a railway! You always need it sooner or later, if only for spares. Thank God he went and now they're pulling it round nicely, you'd like the Isle of Man Line, it stopped developing in the 1920s, so it's still a wonderful survival from the Victorian/Edwardian era.

Railway people love talking about other railways, but they are very careful not to criticise, almost

Right: 'Merddin Emrys' *leaves the shadow of the waste slate tip as it passes the slate miners' cottages on its way to Blaenau Ffestiniog.*

10
W

superstitiously so, in the same way that I have noticed jazz musicians will very rarely go on record disliking *anyone* else's playing. Oh yes, they will be very rude about what a certain manager is doing to a line, or a current shortsighted policy, or mistakes in the past, but the line itself is a sacred animal. I once heard the Talyllyn being praised up to the skies as perfectly organised, highly maintained and beautifully run. – 'And totally boring,' added some wag. The rest were immediately down on him like a ton of bricks. The Talyllyn Railway, of course, was the pioneer in steam revival and to insult it is akin to blasphemy, and it would be almost as hard to be unkind to the Festiniog. How can you be rude about a place where Jo Clulow can casually pull a sheet of paper out of a drawer and say: 'Now, here's an 1882 drawing of a wheel that we're using to build our new Fairlie engine ....' The sense of history is almost overpowering. There are even poignant touches of modern history here, as in a tiny run-around engine tucked in one corner made by the Burton-on-Trent firm of Baguley and Drewry.

'Part of a special order made recently for Mozambique railways,' says Jo laconically. 'The order was cancelled after they'd been made. They got no money. Went bankrupt. We picked up one second-hand.'

Railways are like onions, layer inside layer, and although Boston Lodge was a private empire within

Right: *The breathtaking approach to Tanygrisiau station along the side of the North Wales and Tanygrisiau reservoir.*

Below: *Leaving the hills behind,* 'Merddin Emrys' *follows the edge of Afon Dwyrd valley on its way to Penrhyn.*

DDUALLT

Left: *A stop at Dduallt halt to pick up some footsore hikers.*

the larger universe of the railway, there turned out to be an inner temple here, inside which even Jo did not care to go.

'Like to have a look at Dan Wilson and his telephone kingdom?' he said. 'Because if you do, I'm not coming in with you. Don't want to bring my dirt in your place, Dan,' he added, as the high priest came out and ushered me back in, and fled. Inside, after the heat and dark and scraps and dirt of the shed, it was blindingly clean and white. It was the Festiniog Railway's own telephone exchange, and Dan, long-time editor of the *Festiniog* magazine and a telecommunications engineer in his own right, was the Wizard of Oz in there. There was no noise at all, except for odd little chattering and whirring sounds, like the old-style airport departure boards where all the signs cascaded for a while till they found the right destination. Chatter, chatter, whirr, whirr – every bunch of sounds represented two people ringing each other. Multiple thoughts and conversations were passing through this very room. It was like being inside a brain.

'Some of this is really quite old equipment,' said Dan.

'Needs replacing, you mean?'

'Oh no,' said Dan shocked. 'I mean, it's rare and ancient. Of course, you get some pedants who say that I shouldn't mix up the old stuff and the newer stuff.'

'Pedants,' I said. 'You mean, there are phone preservationists like there are railway preservationists?'

'Of course. There's the world of phone fans and the world of old phone fans, and we get both sorts in here.'

A new concept opened up for me. Phone fans. Phone phreaks. And Dan was one, tucked away where he couldn't see or smell an engine.

'Do you mean that when you go to another railway, the first thing you look at is their telephone system?'

'Well, of course,' said Dan, as if dealing with a child. 'What else? We've got about the best one there is, with 270 phones and six exchanges, though I have to admit that the Severn Valley Railway is about level pegging with us.'

'When I was there' I told him, 'they did tell me about a man who had joined the line simply to work the phones.'

'I think it's a Mr Bradbury, but I've never actually met him. Anyway, we two are definitely the leading lines, though the old North Yorkshire Moors doesn't do badly, and I've heard that the Swanage people are doing a lot.'

'Can you actually hear what people are saying?'

'Certainly, if you want to. That one over there, for instance, is Tanybwlch trying to get through to Blaenau. Just wait a minute. And failing. And dialling again. Now, just plug this in and have a listen.'

He gave me a red phone. I put it to my ear.

'Hello, is that you, Norman?'

'It's for someone called Norman,' I said.

'Ah!' said Dan. 'Just the very chap I've been trying to get hold of all morning.' He flicked a switch. 'Norman? Dan here – just happened to be listening in. Look, the thing is....'

Why do I have such a strong image of that scene in the silent inner sanctum, without a sniff of railways about it? I think it's something to do with the sight of a man playing God, intercepting messages, answering prayers. Everyone in a railway is in charge of some little layer of the onion, everyone is allowed to have a walk-on part and a few lines in the big production. Everyone you see walking round a railway is playing God to a smaller or lesser extent, but on the Festiniog line it's even more so, because the Festiniog is the Old Testament of narrow gauge, a promised land set in the midst of the unbelieving Welsh.

2 It's a Long, Long Way to Bishops Lydeard

The West Somerset Railway

When Mr Douglas Hill took over as the manager of the West Somerset Railway in 1981, the first thing that happened was that he was fired.

'After I had been there about three months, the Board called me in to a meeting and said that the railway was in such a bad shape that they couldn't afford to keep me on. They were sorry, and they didn't know what to do next, and they just hoped I would stay long enough to sketch out a programme to take them into the next year.'

As it turned out, Mr Hill's advice was so valued that the railway never quite parted with him, he never really left, and he is still there as manager nearly ten years on. But it was a close thing. In 1981 West Somerset Railway came nearer to closing down and going under than any preserved line has done – as far as I can make out, no preserved line *has* ever collapsed, with the possible exception of the Derwent Valley line, and several score of experts have told me why that doesn't count, though I could never quite follow their reasoning.

Either way, Mr Hill felt pretty depressed. He had come from industry with a safe background in work study, and here he was about to study his own lack of work. Quite why the railway was in such bad shape is a matter of argument. One history states flatly that it was over-extended by opening up too much of the line closed by BR too quickly. Another theory is that the deal signed by the railway with Somerset County Council, whereby the council owned it and the railway rented itself back from the SCC, meant a slow outpouring of lifeblood in the shape of rent. Mr Hill himself seems to think that dozy management and an inability to get on with either the council or the local farmers had something to do with it. But in 1981, only five years after the line had reopened, there wasn't much point in standing around wondering who to blame. Something had to be done.

It was pretty drastic, recalls Mr Hill. The workforce, which stood at twenty permanent staff, was pruned back to only four. The amount of steam on the line, more expensive than other services, was cut back sharply in favour of diesel. (British Rail must have chuckled at this.) They eliminated most of the winter service. They did a crash programme on cost-effectiveness and took a long hard look at those engines which broke down most often.

Like a country being given a dose of tough anti-inflationary medicine, the railway recovered slowly but consistently through the 1980s until they're now in modest solvency again. Ask Mr Hill about the position at the end of the 1980s, and his face breaks out nearly into a smile.

'Lots of good things are happening. We've got an ex-merchant navy man who's running the engine shed now, and has made all the difference to it. We've bought a large engine shed at Swindon, which was listed as a historic building but had no planned function, and that'll be coming here. We had *Evening Star* on loan this year, which brought a lot of people in, and the weather has been lovely, which brought us a record number of visitors.'

'And there's the prospect of getting into Taunton,' I say.

Previous page: *The Quantock Hills are the setting for ex-Somerset and Dorset Railway loco No. 53808 as it heads along to Bishop's Lydeard.*

Right: 'Evening Star' *travels past the picturesque scenery and farm buildings of Nethercott on its way to Bishop's Lydeard.*

Below: *Inside the cab of* 'Evening Star', *loco No. 92220, the last steam engine built for British Rail at Swindon.*

92220

92220

Everyone says that. People on all the other lines say to me, just wait till the WSR gets back into Taunton. Then it will really go places. But Mr Hill's face falls again.

'Well, that's a long way off. The change of signalling into Taunton would cost £300,000 alone, so British Rail inform us. I'm afraid BR's terms are prohibitive at the moment.'

Reading between the lines, I would guess that BR would do anything to avoid the upheaval of having a branch line, which they once successfully got rid of, come riding back in again. I would also guess that the traumas of 1981 are helping to hold the WSR back; if you have been too far, too fast, once already, you hesitate to do it again. And although it is six miles short of its original length to Taunton, the West Somerset line is still the longest preserved steam line in Britain (not to be confused with the East Somerset, which is about the shortest). It's about twenty miles long, and is said to have more stations in Somerset that British Rail itself does. For a private railway, that's a lot of maintenance, a lot of bridges, thousands of sleepers, nearly fifty miles of fencing....

'I sometimes think it's a bit on the long side as a trip', says Mr Hill suddenly, out of the blue. 'Just a fraction. The steam trip takes seventy eight minutes. I think for the average holidaymaker sixty minutes is about right.'

'You can't make it shorter though, can you?'

'No, but you can put up the speed limit.'

The Mid-Hants Railway, the so-called Watercress Line, are pressing for an upwards revision of the 25 mph speed limit, even though they are a shorter line. Shorter and richer. Mr Hill mentions how much money there is in the Watercress Line, not through any spirit of jealousy, just envy, and because of the complicated equation which governs the location of

Left: 'Evening Star' *runs through the Quantock Hills and the beautiful Somerset countryside.*

Right: *No. 53808 attacking the gradient at Castle Hill near Williton.*

Opposite: *The steam is lost in the summer mist as loco No. 53808 approaches Crowcombe in early morning.*

preserved lines. The West Somerset is a long way from any big conurbation, so it gets *less* in the way of volunteer labour and expertise, and financial backing, but because it has sheer distance to look after, it actually needs *more* than the Watercress Line. It doesn't get it. It doesn't even offer a full steam service, as half the trains are little diesel multiple unit affairs. Why not more steam?

'Good Lord, we couldn't afford to keep more than one engine in steam on one day,' says Mr Hill. 'Expensive stuff, steam.'

But the first day I arrived in 1989 they were cheerful enough. Today, they told me, we are offering a better service than British Rail. More trains, more often. Well, this stood to reason, as it was one of the Wednesdays in 1989 on which there was a national rail strike and if BR are offering no trains at all, then any other railway is well ahead. In fact, you could also have said that on those strike-bound Wednesdays Britain had more steam trains running than any other kind, and no doubt some railway quiz king is already preparing the question: 'When was the last time most of Britain's trains were steam-hauled?' The only man I ever found worried about the British Rail strike was a guard on the Severn Valley Railway who was a full-time BR man in real life, and thus technically strike-busting – at least, he was worried enough about it not to tell me his name.

Below: 'Evening Star' *retires to the Washford sheds.*

In the absence of Taunton, the West Somerset Railway starts at Bishops Lydeard, a comfortable little sandstone town with nice church and an old coaching inn next door, in whose garden I sat with a coffee, deafened by the church bells. Finding the station was the hard bit. There isn't a single sign in the town to the WSR, and I only came across it by accident, just across the main road outside the town and out of sight of the town. When I mentioned this lack of signs to the WSR people, they looked a bit shocked. Nobody *ever* came to the railway via the town, they said; they always came along the main road. It's strange how some towns can be totally divorced from their stations and not make an effort at reconciliation, whereas at somewhere like Minehead, the other end of the line, they are in each other's laps, willy nilly.

Bishops Lydeard and Minehead seem worlds apart. The latter lives by and for the sea, whereas when you set out from Bishops Lydeard and plunge straight into a wood, you get no feeling of the sea being anywhere within 100 miles. In fact you start climbing, which is an odd way to get to the seaside, and for the first four miles it's uphill all the way, through woods and fields and, above all, hilly valleys, the kind of country which we have been trained to think of as typical GWR branch line country, for the very good reason that it was. On a sunny day it is hard to think of anything more beautiful, with the high line of the Quantocks occasionally visible over to the right, the buxom rise and fall of the Devonian landscape all around and over there on the left – according to the official guide – 'the small village of Combe Florey, home of the author Auberon Waugh, whose large house can clearly be seen on the left hand side between the two bridges.'

53806

Above: *Nurtured and blooming: a window box at Stogumber station.*

Above: *Between trains at Williton station.*

Opposite: *Steaming out of Watchet on the return journey to Minehead.*

In other words, it can be briefly glimpsed. Everything is glimpses round here; the countryside is so tight, so neatly packed, that every time you think you are going to get a view, it's taken away from you by another little ridge, rill or outcrop rushing past, another twist as the railway attempts to come to terms with the contours. Never do you get a broad outlook to help you fix yourself in the map of England, and even if you did I suspect it would not be much help, as large settlements are strangely elusive round here. When you stop at Crowcombe you can't see Crowcombe and the same goes for Stogumber (great GWR branch lines names, by the way).

After Crowcombe, top of the line at 400 feet, the train starts easing down through woods and valleys. Is 'easing down' the right word? Owners of railway photograph books will know that there is a special language used in captions to describe the action of steam engines. They never go up a hill, for instance; they 'breast the bank' or 'attack the slope' or even 'storm up the incline'. And never for a moment does the caption writer suggest that a train is having trouble; to our eyes an engine may be making heavy weather of a gradient, but under the photo we will be told that it is 'mounting a spirited assault' on it. And apart from a muscular caption, a photograph of a steam train should also have a plume of smoke contained in it, and smoke is only produced in satisfying quantities if an engine is going uphill, which is why there are so many photos of trains mounting a spirited assault on the heights, and so few of them easing down off the heights. If easing down *is* the correct expression....

After Crowcombe the train eases down to Stogumber, where the station building is on one side of the line, and the platform on the other, which is a bit like having the tower separate from the church, but when you have to build a station on a hillside as you do at Stogumber, that is apparently the easiest way to construct it. After Stogumber there isn't another stop for miles, just more lovely countryside and the sound of the engine bouncing back off the slopes, until we are down on the flat at last and imagining we are about to see the sea. We are not. We have to stop at Williton first. Big place, Williton. Well, anywhere looks big when you haven't seen anything much bigger than Auberon Waugh's house for hours, but Williton seems big because it has the accoutrements of a railway depot, what with water towers, diesel sheds and so on. I am told in confidence that the centre of gravity is gradually passing from Minehead to Williton, and I believe it. Even now, it is the sort of station which every line should have, the station somewhere in the middle where the passenger can get off and stroll down to the engine and stare intelligently at it, before strolling back to your seat; nobody on a steam train seems to go any faster than a stroll, even if you are in danger of missing it.

The next station is called Doniford Beach Halt, so they can't keep the sea from us much longer, and sure enough there it is, all zillion gallons of it, before we arrive at Watchet, the big port on the line. People outside Somerset tend not to have heard of Watchet, but as harbours in North Somerset go, it's big news, and in some ways it's the main reason the line was built at all. The railway used to end here, and from all accounts the effort involved in unloading ships had a touch of high class farce about it. To keep harbour fees low and to catch the tide, ships used to unload at lightning speed, but it wasn't always so easy to get stuff quickly on to the train, as shunting had to be stopped for passenger trains. The main cargo seems to have been esparto grass from Africa for nearby paper mills, all of which had to be packed under waterproof coverings to keep the grass extra dry (it didn't matter if the staff got wet). At peak times, the railway was filled with empty trucks waiting to take the stuff away and staff were drafted in from as far as Taunton to deal with the crush. To look up now, and see the calm round Watchet Harbour, with nothing more active than an angry seagull, makes it hard to imagine that the same space was filled with hypermanic sidings in the old days.

From here the line heads unexpectedly away from

the sea, up a steep climb to Washford and back down to the sealine again at Blue Anchor, and from here it's a virtually straight run along the coast to Minehead, though you could stop and get off at Dunster if you wanted to. The Luttrells did. They lived at Dunster Castle for hundreds of years and were the prime movers in getting the line built to Minehead, so it's only fair if they tended to treat Dunster as their own private station. One could never somehow imagine them living at Minehead. Dunster is an incredibly beautiful historic town, crammed full every day during the season with National Trust-type crowds, while Minehead is much more workaday – a seaside town all right, but geared primarily to the holiday camp and boarding house crowd. On the flat it's all clotted cream teas, and beach windmills, and occasional arcade games, but up the hill at Minehead you also find the old town, quietly holding its breath in an effort not to attract the attention of the crowds. So far it's been lucky.

One of the oddest visitors to Minehead was the *Duchess of Hamilton,* which some would say was the finest steam engine running in Britain today. But it was only rescued by the whim of Billy Butlin, the holiday camp king, who bought it in the 1960s and stuck it in the middle of Minehead camp for the children to play on and their parents to goggle at, with no thought of running it again. It was finally purchased and taken away for a restoration, like a Van Gogh that someone has been using as a dartboard, and now lives a pampered life at York. Seeing the handsome *Evening Star* in action on the line in 1989, I suppose it's not impossible that the *Duchess* might return one day as a guest engine. Yes, she'd say; I used to come on holiday to Minehead ... it was quite nice, but my dear, the people....

It all seems a long way from Bishops Lydeard. It really is quite a journey from one end to the other, helped a lot by the terrain; twenty miles in Somerset is a lot further than twenty miles across, say, a fen or flatland, and a lot more varied. I suppose that's why so many film companies have chosen to film here, perhaps most famously of all, the railway sequences in the Beatles' film *A Hard Day's Night,* though it comes as a slight shock to realise that that must have been well before steam was restored, during British Rail's last days of tenure. We sometimes think of BR as having always been in charge, but come to think of it, in another ten years time the West Somerset Railway will have been in charge longer than BR ever was. Before BR, of course, it was GWR, and before GWR it was the B & ER (Bristol and Exeter Railway).

Above: 'Evening Star' *shunting at Bishop's Lydeard in preparation for the return trip to Minehead.*

Opposite: *Ex-Somerset and Dorset loco No. 53808 at Stogumber station.*

Above: *Retired signalman, Mr Horne, with his wife at Stogumber station.*

I would rather not go into the history of the line. It is, frankly, a little dull. I would rather go back up the line to Stogumber and get off there with my bicycle. I took my bicycle with me on all these trips and apart from the Keighley and Worth Valley Railway, the West Somerset line was the only one that let me take it on for free. And I wanted to get off at Stogumber because Alain le Garsmeur, who took all the photographs for which you bought this book, told me that there was a delightful old couple there to whom I should talk.

I wasn't prepared for quite how old, in railway terms, they were. Mr and Mrs Harry Horne had been involved with this line since 1919. He had worked on it all his life, and now, well past retirement, they still came out to look after the station, show people round, care for the tiny museum area and encourage people to join their support group, the Friends of Stogumber Station. It must, in many ways, be a difficult thing for him to do, because if you have ever worked full-time for a big railway, there is bound to be something rather depressing about coming back to see it run by a bunch of, comparatively, amateurs.

Opposite: *A perfect morning for loco No. 53808's run along the Somerset coast.*

The most startling instance of this occurs in a marvellous book by John Winton about the Festiniog Line. *The Little Wonder: 150 years of the Festiniog Railway* (Michael Joseph, 1986), which records that when the line was revived in the 1950s there was one man, Robert Evans, who was still caretaking there, having joined the line as long ago as 1894. The newcomers, the revivalists, hailed him as a living link with the past, a sort of holy blessing on their invasion, and in 1954 gave him a slap up tea as a tribute. But Winton quotes from a Festiniog railway magazine a rather moving passage to show that that was not at all how Robert Evans saw things.

> 'We remember him, later, as a solitary figure, sad in carpet slippers amid the sparrows and green ruination of the Harbour Station, murmuring unhappily: 'I am afraid ... it has gone too far ... the track ... trains cannot now be run.' To speak plainly, this was not the sort of stuff we wanted to hear, and after a short interval this humble old man who had given his life to our line was eased off the stage – gently and honourably, to be sure, but off the stage.
>
> 'Mr Evans's big trouble, of course, was that he knew too much; he had seen the Festiniog run properly. Railway preservation is rather like marriage in that the bitter knowledge of sordid truths essential to make it work is inimical to the zest and optimism with which it must be entered into. In those two wobbly lines of wet rust across the Cob, Robert Evans saw the raddled husk of a 60-year liaison; we saw them twinkle with the beckoning promise of a new life and, starry-eyed, blundered into the unknown.'

Perhaps because I am unused to finding such fine writing in railway surroundings, this has always convinced me that old railway servants were unreconstructed nostalgics. Harry Horne disproved this. Nothing sentimental about him. He had worked

53808

through the GWR and BR days and didn't want them back; he was just glad that there were some WSR days to live through. At the same time he felt, like an old soldier in peacetime, that things were not run as tightly as they could be. As we sat in the sunshine on Stogumber station a train came up the line from Minehead and echoed off towards Bishops Lydeard, audible long after it had vanished; he pointed after it, frowning.

'There was a handle not turned back on one of those doors. Dangerous, that. If I were still a signalman, I'd have given seven bells ahead of that. It's a signal to the next place to do an external examination.'

I hadn't noticed a single thing. Does he always automatically check trains when they pass?

'Well, it's the habit of a lifetime. I still look at every train without really realising it to see if the taillamp is on the last coach.'

Ignorant question from me: What would it mean if it wasn't there?

'That the last coach was missing of course. Actually, they're very good on this railway now, considering, very good, but you still see things you shouldn't see. The other day, on a station whose name I won't mention, I saw some four-wheel trolleys, the kind where you have to lift up the handle in order to apply the brake. Well, the handles were down – and the trolleys were facing sideways to the line! Oh dear, dear.'

This was not the cry of a man who sees terrible accidents happening; it is the protest of a man who has been brought up to honour the regulations automatically, the outcry of the railway grammarian against a split infinitive. I asked him if in fact in his long signalling career he had ever seen any serious accidents.

'Three,' he replied promptly. 'Not on this line, but on the main line. One was near Powderham Castle, where I was signalman, and one day after a train had gone through I found I couldn't get my up signal back to caution. Funny, I thought, so I went to have a look. What I didn't know was that a fellow had committed suicide just up the line by jumping on the track; all I knew was that I suddenly found these legs thrashing around in my wires. Well, that was really quite dangerous, getting mixed up in the signals like that, and I had to move quite fast to get him out.

'Second time was in a station, when a railwayman who was quite experienced and should have known better, stepped out of the way of one train into the path of another. It took him right along the far platform, and there were these red stains for days and days; collecting him up took a while, too. The third time was when an inspector got his belt caught....'

I'm not particularly squeamish but I had to interrupt him there; the sunny calm day seemed quite at variance with this trench warfare. Did *he* not feel squeamish at all?

'Oh no, not at all. I was trained as an ambulanceman, St John Ambulance. A lot of us were. The GWR liked that, because if you were medically trained, they got a better deal on the insurance premiums for us, and we got certain perks. So you'll find that a lot of old railwaymen volunteered for first aid work.'

Opposite: *After a day by the sea, passengers climb aboard the train for Bishop's Lydeard at Doniford Beach Halt.*

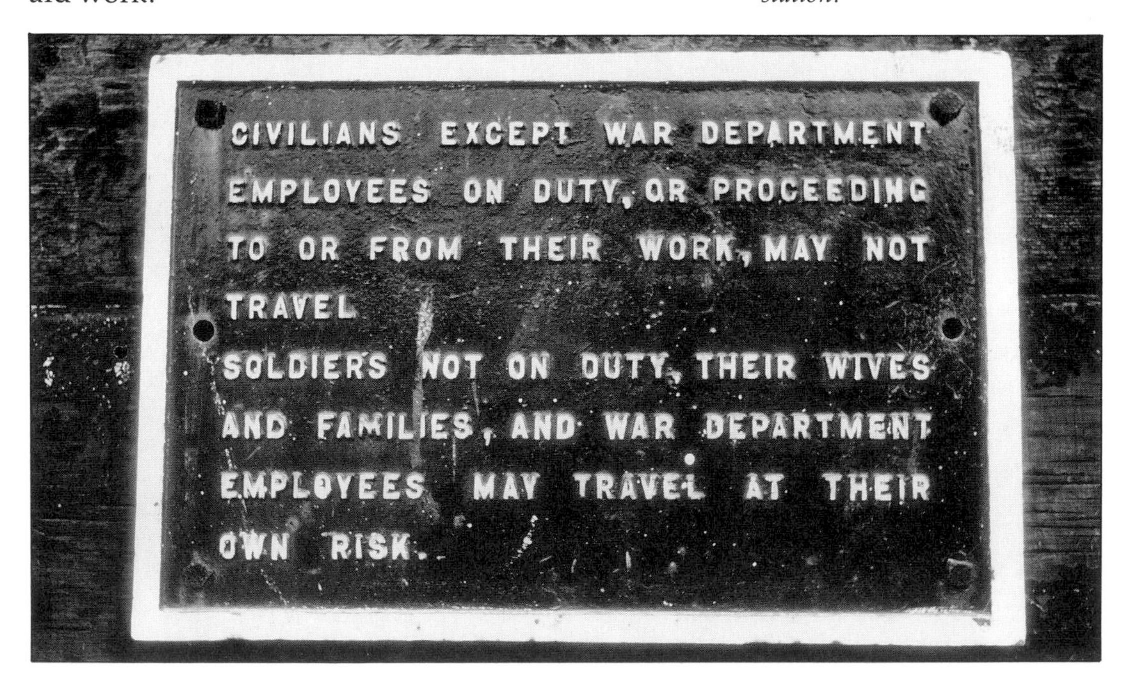

Below: *A reminder of the railway's history – a War Department notice at Williton station.*

Above: *No. 53808 entering Blue Anchor station.*

Opposite: 'Evening Star' *simmering in Minehead station.*

Mr Horne spent some of his working life at Williton Station, and could remember even now the ranks and titles of his colleagues.

'Station master, head porter, *junior* porter, booking clerk, two signalmen, who else, yes, a lorry driver, eight permanent way workers....'

But the staff at Williton Station in the old days was about the same as the entire workforce *now*, wasn't it?

'Yes, coming up to it.'

That's probably why trolleys never got left, brakeless, side-on to the track. It also explains why the railways could act as common carrier, that is, why they were legally obliged to carry anything you asked them to, and why they could carry out all requests. They had the manpower.

'Lions, elephants, anything – they had to take everything', said Mr Horne. 'They took our son's laundry to Bristol University. In the 1950s, when we were here at Stogumber Station and he was at college, he used to send his dirty laundry back home by train. We would wash it and put it on the 8.10 out of here in the morning. It would be delivered to him by mid-afternoon. Couldn't do that today.'

Was there any other freight in and out of Stogumber apart from dirty laundry?

'Oh yes. Pigeons. Whortleberries, in season. Beer – there was a thriving brewery at Stogumber.'

'The railway was a godsend in 1962,' said Mrs Horne. 'That was the really bad winter, if you remember. All the roads to Minehead were cut off, all of them. The only way to get through was down the line, so we had to keep going. My husband was ordered to work at Williton during that time, so I looked after Stogumber Station all by myself. I sometimes wonder what would have happened if there had been another bad winter during the years the railway was closed. People don't think of these things, you see.'

'Esparto grass.' said Mr Horne suddenly. 'That was another thing they carried. For the paper mills at Silverton. It came ashore at Watchet. But although they were obliged to carry it, they would have lost money at the normal rates, it being so light, so they had a special rate for such things: Bulky in Proportion to Weight.'

I enrolled myself as I left in the Friends of Stogumber Station, which I hope to get into *Who's Who* as my club one day, and pedalled off back towards Bishops Lydeard. Cycling gives you a real insight into the gradients of a country, and it was with some relief that I saw the village of Combe Florey heave into sight. I am also a member of another exclusive organisation, the Vague Acquaintances of Auberon Waugh, so I cycled up his drive and fell off exhausted. There was a great commotion of birds somewhere behind me.

'The ducks normally get fed about now,' said a lady approaching me. 'They are given their food by a man on a bicycle, and they probably thought it was you. Who are you, actually?'

I turned out to be Miles Kington, she turned out to be Waugh's secretary, and Waugh turned out to be in London, where he usually is most of the week, so over a cup of tea on the lawn I promised to try and get this

92220
83
B

detail added to the mention of Mr Waugh's large house in the West Somerset Railway guide, so that passengers should not wave or even gawp at his house unnecessarily on days when he was working in Soho.

'We love having the trains come past,' she told me. 'It's wonderful to see the plume of smoke at the end of the vista, though I must say that some engines seem to have more trouble with the slope than others.'

No, no, they're not having trouble with the slope – they are mounting a brave assault on it. In a sense, that is what the West Somerset Railway is doing too. I talked to a man before we started this book who saw all steam railways in terms of wine vintages, and who, when we said we probably would not be including the Watercress Line, nodded cautiously.

'It's a lovely line,' he said, 'but it's not mature yet. Give it a few years, and it will have real vintage qualities. Or the Severn Valley. Actually, I sometimes think the Severn Valley may be near its peak, and you never know, it might get a little over-ripe. And if it does, do you know which railway might go ahead of all of them? It sounds crazy, but the West Somerset. They're doing good things there already, and it's got more potential than all of them. I think the West Somerset could be a cracker.'

I'll drink to that.

Right: *Enthusiasts admire ex-Somerset and Dorset loco No. 53808 as it departs from Minehead.*

Left: *The sky is filled with steam after water has been taken at Minehead station.*

53808

3 Beyond the End of the Line

The West Highland Extension Line

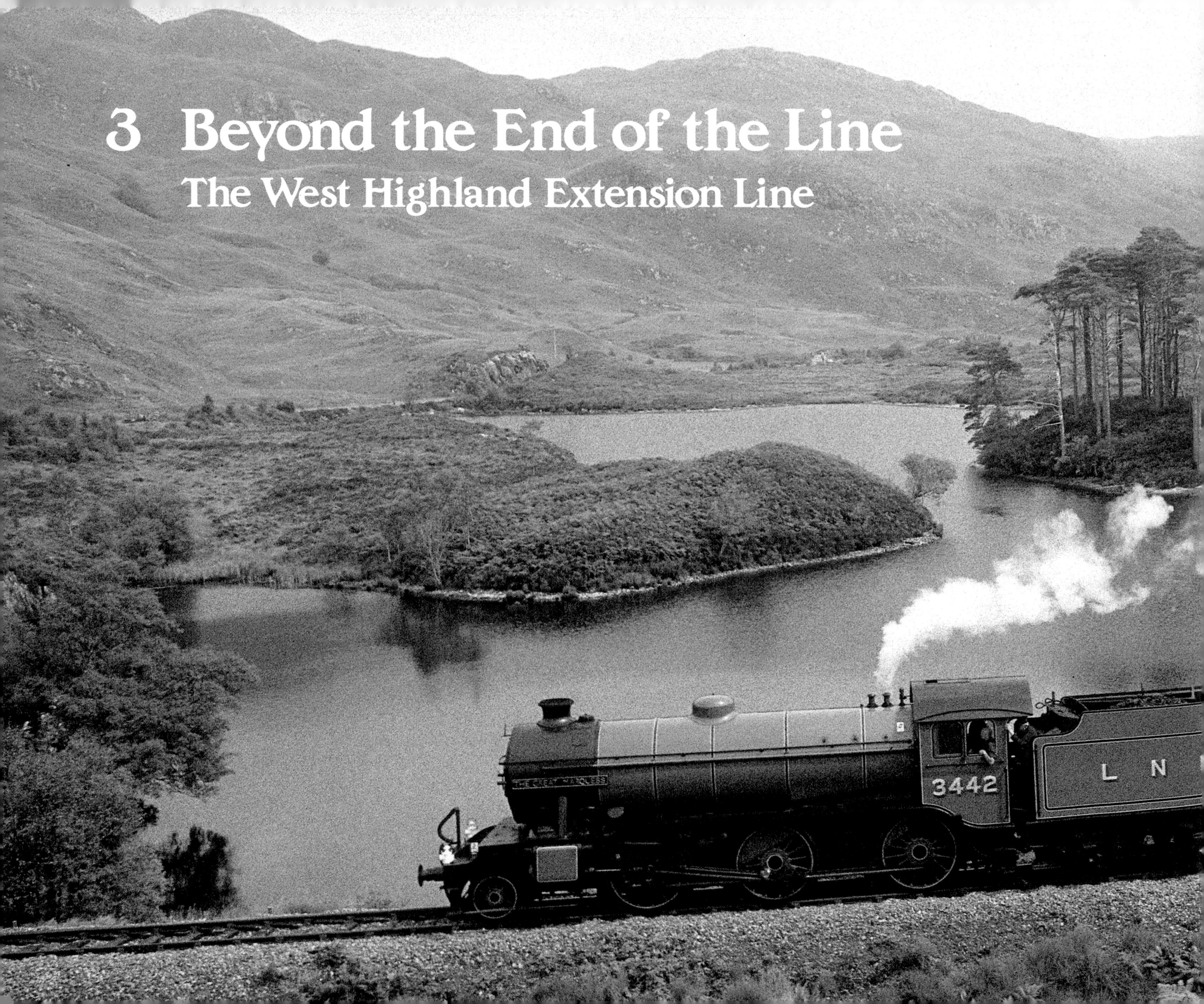

West Highland Line

WORKING on the BBC television series *Steam Days* in 1986 as a presenter I discovered how many people there were in Britain who knew more about trains than I did. That was fine by me; I didn't really want to know that much. But I did learn one thing, and that was the further you got from London, the more relaxed people on British Rail became and freer from bureaucracy. (The same thing was true, oddly enough, of BBC television film crews.) The furthest we got was Mallaig, at the end of the West Highland line, and of all the people we dealt with, none was nicer or less liable to abide by the rule-book than the railway people between Fort William and Mallaig. 'You'd hardly think it was part of BR at all half the time,' we were told, 'it's almost like an independent railway.'

The same was true when I went back in 1989 for this book; the volunteers down in the freight depot said to me, admiringly, that up here they did things their own way and only listened to London with half an ear. This is not the normal attitude to British Rail. Oh, all railway enthusiasts are behind British Rail to a man, because if you are pro-railway you are by definition pro-British Rail, but having said that, railway enthusiasts will also comment at length on how obstructive, unimaginative, greedy, slow-footed, uncooperative, bureaucratic and narrow-minded BR can be (though don't get me wrong – they are behind British Rail all the way...). I could give you examples of how the Mallaig Line tends to be broad-minded, but London might phone up and put a stop to it, so I won't.

What stands out a mile is that the only section of British Rail that runs regular summer steam services – and remember that British Rail for a long time said they would never let steam back on their lines again, never – is one of the furthest from London. There are steam specials in England, big gala outings now and then, but no regular day in, day out steam services *down in the timetable* except on the Mallaig line, where they take it in their stride, no problem. Perhaps it's the independent, self-sufficient feeling you get from being at the end of the line where you have to look after yourself a bit, because Mallaig is not just at the end of the line, it's beyond the end of the line.

That's because the West Highland Line proper ends at Fort William, a hundred miles north of Glasgow, a hundred miles of the bleakest and most beautiful scenery you'll find anywhere. It passes along the sides of Loch Lomond, soon after leaving Glasgow, but you are far more likely to remember the desolate heights of Rannoch Moor and the weaving of the line round the flanks of the bare mountains. Once, driving across Rannoch Moor, I stopped the car when there was no traffic about to fill my ears with the sounds of the moor: the distant birds, the whispering of the wind in the grass and so on. There was not even that to be heard. On a summer afternoon, when nature is supposedly getting on with things, there was literally nothing to be heard, only blank emptiness, like a ghost town after the ghosts have departed. So it comes as a delicious relief to descend the last twenty or thirty miles through wooded glens, alongside rushing rivers, to Fort William at the head of Loch Linnhe.

Previous page: *Class K4 2-6-0, No. 3442,* 'The Great Marquess' *skirts the west end of Loch Eilt.*

Right: *Through the viaduct,* 'The Great Marquess' *makes the steep climb up to Glenfinnan station.*

Below: *Passengers crossing the lines at Arisaig station to catch the Fort William train.*

3442
LNER

And that might always have been the end of the line, were it not that a hundred years ago Parliament was much concerned about the terrible plight of the crofters who lived beyond Fort William, down to the coast. They received reports of their starvation and hopelessness much as Britain hears about famine in the Third World today. In 1890, the Third World was in north-west Scotland. Parliament wrung its hands and asked what it could do. Build a railway line to the coast, came one answer, and let the fishing folk get their produce down south and make some money. So the West Highland Line Extension, as it was unromantically called, was constructed in the 1890s, the first railway line ever to get a government subsidy.

The big problem, apart from blasting it through the hills, was where to build it to. There was no town on the coast opposite Fort William, hardly a village. So they found a dot on the map which seemed to have a nice bit of anchorage by it, discovered that it was called Mallaig and built the line to it. The place was, literally, created by the railway. The day before the line opened, it took seven or eight hours to get to Arisaig and Mallaig by horse and wagon. The day after the line opened, it took an hour by train. It must have seemed like Concorde replacing balloons overnight.

The extraordinary thing was that while doing the television series we found someone in Fort William who remembered the line being built – the Mallaig extension, that is. The work was started in 1897 and finished in 1901, but Mr Kennedy, now in his nineties, could well remember the work starting in the last century. We rushed a camera round to his house and I interrogated the last living survivor about those days, but not unnaturally there was little of interest that he could remember, any more than you or I would remember about a new road being built near our birthplace. What he really wanted to talk about was the 1920s, when he had been a Highland Games champion. There on the walls of his sitting-room were photos of him as a handsome young man, not just tossing the caber but putting the shot and, I believe, throwing the hammer.

Above: *Taking on more passengers at the well-kept station of Mallaig.*

'We got around in those days,' said Mr Kennedy, 'from Games to Games. Between us, we made a few bob. Amateurs did quite well for themselves, even then.'

I wanted to know how cabers were transported from one event to another, or whether you had to use the resident log, but of course the television producer had switched off by this time. Fascinating though these memories were, if it wasn't about railways, it wasn't worth having, and so it was all lost to posterity. He was not even mentioned in the film, and the only image I retain of him now is of a pair of twinkling eyes, the old newspaper cuttings and the anecdotes of athletes on the road round the Highlands.

There were, however, two sterling people in the film. One was the driver, Willie Corrigan, whose soft Scottish voice on the sound-track insisted that the Mallaig line was the finest in the world, that he never got tired of it and that it was different every time. No matter that, in my experience, *every* driver tells you

Opposite: *Bound for Fort William,* 'The Great Marquess' *crosses the viaduct at the head of Loch-nam-Uamh.*

25

the same about *his* line; they always patently mean it, and it is always moving to hear them say it.

The other was William McAlpine, well-known as a railway enthusiast and member of the McAlpine engineering family, who could only have time to appear in the programme if we paid for him to be flown up by helicopter for the day. He duly arrived by helicopter (which was commandeered by a happy producer for overhead shots of steam trains) and talked to us about the line. On any other line he would have been quite interesting; here, he was in his element, because the line had been built by his family. Robert McAlpine, who was so in love with concrete that they called him 'Concrete Bob', had made this the first major exercise in concrete anywhere in the world, and even today, when Bill McAlpine stood patting Glenfinnan Viaduct, the concrete pride of the line, as if he were patting a family horse, and said: 'When *we* built this,' the pride was as touching as that of Willie Corrigan.

He told us the story of Robert's son, Malcolm, who worked on the line as a young engineer and was desperately wounded by flying debris from an explosion – shattered ribs, fractured pelvis, punctured abdomen. The distraught father, when he was told the news in Glasgow, dragged a top surgeon all the way up to Fort William in the middle of the night to do an operation the next day, followed by an agonising journey on an improvised rail stretcher train back south. It occurred to me after making the film that my Aunt Peggy, who had been married into the McAlpine family for a while, might have come across Malcolm in later life. I asked her. She had.

'I don't remember anything about him building railways,' she said, 'but I do remember that he had this awful scar on his stomach. He was a bit of a one for the girls, you know, and even in later life he used to fascinate and horrify them by unbuttoning his shirt and getting them to put their hand in the wound. Naughty old boy, he was.' She chuckled at the memory. I goggled at the thought that my own aunt had once touched the famous wound.

So it was with a slight feeling of belonging to the line that I returned in 1989 to the scene of our film. Illusory, no doubt, but a small bundle of memories always entitles you to harbour the illusion. It didn't survive my return long. When I set out to find Mr Kennedy again, I could find no one who had even heard of him. Oldest survivor? Don't recall anyone like that. Do you, Jim? No, not me. Willie Corrigan, the driver who had talked us through the film, had died in 1988. So, come to that, had my Aunt Peggy, my faint link with Concrete Bob.

But memories do not fade that fast in Fort William. In the library in the town there was an exhibition to mark the centenary of the conception of the railway from Glasgow. Half of it was the kind of exhibition you'd expect; maps of the line, pictures of old trains, a bit of history, a bit of scenery. The other half was utterly simple but totally unexpected; it was a long display of snapshots of people who had worked on the line. No matter if the photos of the grinning groups were out of focus, tilted or slightly crumpled, they

Opposite: 'The Great Marquess' *crosses the spectacular Glenfinnan Viaduct as it heads for Mallaig.*

Below: 'The Great Marquess', *tender first, ready for its return to Fort William.*

provided a panorama of the last fifty years of people on the line. Underneath each photo they had written in the names if they knew them and left a blank if they didn't, with an invitation to visitors to write in any names they knew, and gradually, in dozens of different hands, the identification was building up, even if sometimes people could only remember first names and wrote 'Fred (?)'. The whole thing betokened a real sense of railway community, which I doubt you would find on many other lines these days.

Outwardly, not much has changed on the line. Ben Nevis still frowns hugely down on Fort William at one end, and the sea spreads out from Mallaig at the other, full of islands like a war fleet getting ready for inspection. I can't help feeling that Ben Nevis has been put in the wrong place, though. The largest mountain in Scotland should not be beside the sea; it should be the highest peak in a series of peaks, so that it looks as tall as it really is. Poised over Fort William, with no fellow peaks standing by, it gives no sense of its true height, like a 6′ 7″ rugby forward standing in a room all by himself. Still, it's far too late to move it now, and it is undeniably impressive to move away from Fort William with that great mass of green and brown hanging over you. The first few times I travelled out to Fort William I was goggling at the mountain so much that I failed to notice the flight of locks which marks the start of the Caledonian Canal, the great waterway across Scotland which was out of date before it was even finished.

What you have to bear in mind when you're setting off from Fort William to Mallaig is that you're going from sea level to sea level. Loch Linnhe, the water from which the town is separated by a dangerous dual carriageway, is the tip of a twenty-mile finger from the sea which is not quite useful enough to support a thriving coastal ferry service. The trip to Mallaig is like going across the back of a glove – you go a long way up and a long way down but every now and again you glimpse a long finger of water snaking down to the sea. I think it is this co-existence of wild mountain scenery and the invisible nearness of the sea which

Above: *The driver of* 'The Great Marquess' *surveys Mallaig station.*

Above: *A young steam buff climbs aboard* 'The Great Marquess' *at Mallaig.*

Opposite: 'The Great Marquess' *curving through Morar on its way to Fort William with the South Morar hills behind.*

gives the Mallaig line a special flavour that you don't get on the line up from Glasgow or indeed on the Settle – Carlisle line, which are upland lines pure and simple. The Mallaig line gives you the same feeling that you get when about to break out of mist into sunshine, the same sensation of being on the edge of surprise.

The Caledonian Canal is a surprise. The huge aluminium works at Corpach, just beyond, are a surprise. The herons on the loch there are a surprise and so is the brightness of the rowan berries, like fruit on top of a wild cocktail. It also comes as a surprise to learn that Corpach and Fort William, though barely a mile apart, were once deadly enemies.

'Oh yes,' the local girl with the refreshment trolley told me, as we rose towards Glenfinnan, 'there was a time when if a Fort William girl went out with a fellow from Corpach she'd get beaten up. And so would he.'

'Does this still happen?'

'Oh no!' she said, surprised at my naivety. 'This was all a long time ago.'

'Good,' I said.

'Nowadays it's Fort William and Mallaig,' she continued. 'If all the Mallaig boys come to a Fort William disco, there's *always* a punch-up afterwards. Even my boyfriend doesn't like it if he sees me just talking to a Mallaig boy and I always get a real earful. Stupid, isn't it? The reason is that Fort William people look down on Mallaig people as country bumpkins, so of course there's trouble. But Mallaig people aren't country bumpkins at all.'

'No?'

'No. It's the Ballachulish people who are the bumpkins. Mark you, to be fair, the Glasgow people look down on us at Fort William as yokels.'

And, she might have added, Edinburgh people often look down on Glaswegians, and so it goes on until you get New Yorkers looking down on Londoners. By this time we had arrived at Glenfinnan which is a stiff climb from Loch Eil. Here is the great viaduct built by my ex-relation-by-marriage. Here come tourists by the coachload. It is not, however, to

see the viaduct. They come because the Scots have a curious habit of ignoring their great achievements and dwelling on their glorious defeats, and the tall memorial and visitor centre to which they come are there to commemorate the landing of Bonnie Prince Charlie prior to his disastrous 1745 attempt to corner the market for the Stuart family. And although we are always invited to view him as a dashing, romantic figure (which is hard if you have ever seen a picture of his fat, bald shape in later life), I am more and more disposed to see him as the first of the yuppies, making a hash of his first big foreign posting.

If John Barnes had his way, there would be another attraction here, the Glenfinnan Station Museum. In 1986 the station and signal box were thriving, and we were able to film the signalman at work in his gleaming box. Now, it is all shut down, empty and damp. These days we have a compulsion to reopen anything shut down, empty and damp as a museum, and Mr Barnes has some imaginative ideas as to how it can be done, but he seems very quiet on the subject of one attraction: midges. I noticed that as the signalman left his box prior to filming, he smeared a thick layer of cream on his face. I couldn't think why. Minutes later when a thick river of insects landed on my face and started crawling everywhere they could find an entry, I understood. One of the best-selling books in Scotland in 1989 was *'Midges in Scotland'* by Professor George Hendry, and any Englishman who has encountered the little beasts will not find them funny.

Right: *A panoramic view of Loch-nam-Uamh as* 'The Great Marquess' *crosses the viaduct.*

Below: *The classic view of the West Highland Line* – 'The Great Marquess' *steaming towards Mallaig.*

L N E R
3442

L N E R

They are, apparently, worse at Glenfinnan than almost anywhere, and my advice to Mr Barnes would be not to play them down but to make a feature of them: WE HAVE SEEN THE MIDGES AT GLENFINNAN stickers, at the very least.

Not only has the signal box closed down, but signalling has almost closed down. The line is now radio-controlled. Every driver has a two-way radio in his cab, so that he can not only receive orders but hear every other driver in his panel between Mallaig and Tyndrum. (There's another panel between Tyndrum and Glasgow.) They built a special mast for transmissions high up in the mountains and every driver I spoke to agreed that when the system worked, it was wonderful, far superior to conventional signals. They all agreed that when it didn't work it was a disaster. Because the mast was not built in the right place, it was suggested to me, and because BR didn't buy the most expensive walkie-talkies they might have done, breakdowns were not uncommon, and then it was a question of a weary trudge along the line to the nearest phone. One man even hinted to me that drivers might be tempted to go through sections without a token, which is so unthinkable that I must have misheard him.

On through an enclosed valley sprayed with birch trees and grand exposed rocks, like the ribs of a cathedral showing through, over the watershed and down a magnificent green ramp to the side of Loch Eilt (Loch Eil, Loch Eilt, Lochailort ... all the names hereabouts seem to come from the same Scrabble hand) which in some ways is the handsomest part of the whole country, which is what you tend to say about every section as you come to it. You'd think that a countryside so damp and green would be free of the dangers of summer fires from steam engines, but just to be on the safe side British Rail send out two trains at

Left: 'The Great Marquess' *working its way under the rocky crags on the south side of Loch Eilt.*

Right: 'The Great Marquess' *follows the bank of Loch Eilt on its way to Mallaig.*

L N E R

the start of every steam season. The first has a steam engine and lots of sparks. The second, twenty minutes behind, has lots of beaters aboard with big brooms, ready to put out any fires started by the first. 1988 was a bad year for fires. 1989 wasn't.

The steam service in summer is organised fairly simply. British Rail pay the owners of the engine some £400 a day for the hire of it. They fill a train with several hundred enthusiasts and make a healthy profit. And the driving of the engine falls to a BR driver such as Callum MacRaild who comes of such a railway family that when he told me he had eight uncles on the trains, I didn't question it. He worked all through the steam era here on the Mallaig line, but the irony is that he never drove a train until now.

'Aye, well, not officially. I was a fireman for fifteen years, because promotion moved awfully slowly in the old days, but for several years I fired for my brother, who was a driver, and he let me do a good lot of the driving. I was just about to take my steam test when they announced the withdrawal of steam, so it hardly seemed worth it. And now here I am driving steam again. It's great. Of course, it's not quite like in the old days when a driver had a one-man, one-engine relationship. You heard about drivers who gave up their Sundays just to go and polish their engines, or who even bought their own oil because they didn't think the company oil was good enough. That had all gone by the time I joined in 1948, but I tell you what – these old blokes are reincarnated today as the volunteers who come up here to Fort William and look after the steam engines. Those fellows will clamber in anywhere, do anything, get dirty all over. Well, it's lovely for me. I turn up, the engine's all ready, and off I go. I come back and they take it away. No steam driver ever had such luxury.'

But even being a jockey with his own stable boys to do the work does not blind him to the advantages of modern engines.

'I'm not against diesels at all. It's easier to hear these new radios in a diesel, for a start. And I'd far rather be caught in a snowstorm in a diesel!'

Above: 'The Great Marquess' *shunting on the outskirts of Mallaig.*

Like all drivers up here, Callum has great stories about being caught in snow, but that would make a separate book.

'Even those new Sprinters aren't bad. Only thing is, you don't feel you're actually driving a train. It's more like a bus. But you ought to try one.'

And I did, and that's how I came to meet the girl with the service trolley, who had never been on the steam train and wasn't looking forward to it as it was said to be very crowded and difficult for trolleys to negotiate. She chatted with me until Lochailort and then said: 'Well, better see what the captain wants to drink,' and she moved forward to the driver's door and put her head round, for all the world like a stewardess offering the pilot the run of the duty-free. Something else you don't get on a steam engine.

The final run down to Mallaig is, like every other bit, the best bit of the journey, with an enormous prospect over the sea to the islands, some close and huge, some hardly visible. The water is dotted with fishing boats, but none of that fish comes by train any

Opposite: *High above the trees* 'The Great Marquess' *crosses the Glenfinnan Viaduct.*

Above: *The permanent way – a view along the River Ailort.*

more, even though the line was built to carry it. It's landed at Mallaig and lorried away, sometimes as far as Spain if it is the delectable langoustine. But in the days when Mallaig was the busiest herring port in Europe, yes, Europe, you could hardly move for fish. It fell out of every boat, every nook and cranny. If you wanted a herring to cook on your shovel on the journey home, said Callum, you didn't ask for one, you just picked one up off the quay. There's the legendary story of the man at the station who asked the driver if there were any spare fish on board. Aye, third car down, he said. The man opened the door to the third car down and ten ton of fish fell on top of him.

'But they were greedy,' said Callum. 'They just fished and fished, and scrapped the sea dry. They almost threw the stuff away. In fact, they did throw the stuff away, because sometimes they overfished and had a surplus of herring and made a special trip to sea to throw it all back in. No wonder the herring vanished.'

Opposite: 'The Great Marquess' *cutting through the highlands at Loch Eilt.*

George Lawrie is the last herring smoker left in Mallaig. When he was a lad (and he's not old now) he can remember having to switch on his bike lights coming back from school in *daylight,* because the smoke from the thirteen or more fish-houses was so thick against the sun. His remaining chimney goes unnoticed. And what is worse, the herring haven't come back, so the fish he smokes have to be brought in by road and taken away again by road. There is actually no reason for him to be by the seaside at all, it seems. There is, to be honest, not a lot at Mallaig to attract the visitor or to keep the railway enthusiast from the return journey. The going and coming is the thing.

Inter City Rail (who, bafflingly, are in charge of the steam service) are well pleased with the profitability of the run and not likely to cancel it. What also seems baffling is that it runs only four times a week. Not on Wednesday, because that's the day the posh Royal Scot comes round. And not on Friday or Saturday. You or I might think that those would be the busiest days, but I am assured by BR that people tend to be driving to or from their holidays on Friday and Saturday, and don't go on steam excursions.

So at the moment we have the strange situation or BR running a steam service which is usually fully booked in advance (no turn up and get on) but which they do not plan to expand. More trains? I asked. No room in the timetable they said. The upshot is that they carry 18,000 steam passengers a year, which by a long way is far below all the other lines in this book. Even the Isle of Mull line, barely one and three-quarter miles of narrow gauge across the water somewhere, takes 24,000 people a year. Extraordinary.

Not that Mike Thompson or Jim Coleman would care. They are the two volunteers I found in the Fort William freight depot, a wild place with men loading vast log lorries and a mini-cab hut guarded by savage dogs. They were lavishing love and attention on a Black 5, made in Crewe in 1945, No. 44871, and as long as there are enough passengers to keep the service going, that's all they need. One of them is a cancer

L N E R
3442

research doctor and the other is a maintenance man, but it was impossible to tell which was which, dressed as they were in the classless garb of the volunteer (blue dungarees, black face, oily rag). They own an engine. Not this one, but No. 2048, a tiny four-wheel engine made in 1948 by Peckett's of Bristol, and their great ambition is to get it running again. It's at Steamtown, at Carnforth. Years of work are needed yet, but one day, given money and effort, it will be gleaming and running.

'And then what?' I ask, always hoping to crack the secret of railway mania.

'How do you mean, then what?' they say.

'What do you do with it then?''

'Well, there's about a mile of track we can take it up and down,' says Jim.

'I have no ambition to drive it,' says Mike. 'I wouldn't mind shovelling coal into it, though.'

I suddenly spot the truth. They don't want to finish it. They just want to work on it. Perhaps rebuilding an engine is a bit like getting to Mallaig; such a wonderful journey that actually getting there is bound to be an anti-climax. A pavement artist once told me that the golden rule in pavement painting is *never* to finish a picture, or people will lose interest. It applies to more than pavement art, it seems.

Above: *Banavie station – with an unusually clear view of Ben Nevis.*

Right: *The end of the line –* 'The Great Marquess' *pulls into the station at Mallaig.*

Skye Ferry
Ind Est
Town Centre B8008

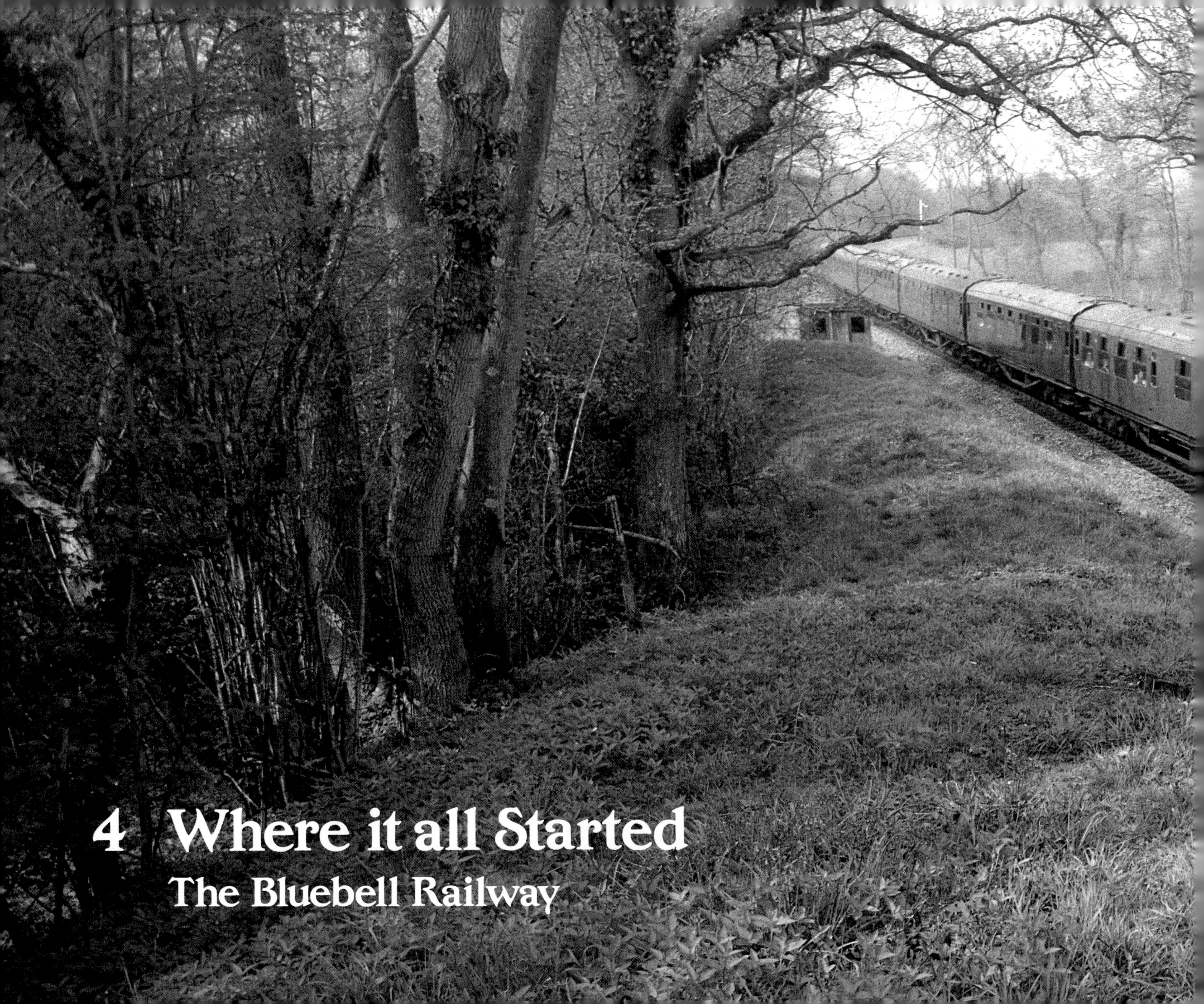

4 Where it all Started

The Bluebell Railway

SOUTHERN
1618

Previous page: *Bluebells by the Bluebell Line – a Southern class U 2-6-0, No. 1618, heads towards Sheffield Park.*

Opposite: *Merchant Navy class 4-6-2 loco No. 35027, 'Port Line', climbs towards Horsted Keynes.*

THE ONLY honest thing to say about the Bluebell Railway is that it goes from nowhere to nowhere in the middle of nowhere, but as that is not likely to make me many friends I shall say something else instead. I shall say that it reminds me of a brick wall I once built.

My first wife, a keen gardener, thought that it would be nice to have a small raised flowerbed in our tiny garden in Ladbroke Grove, but as she was not a keen bricklayer she thought it would be a nice idea if I built it. I had never built anything out of bricks, so I had no idea if I was a keen bricklayer or not, but as the space enclosed was to be only five feet by two, and the wall was to be hardly two feet high, I could see no real objection. In any case, there are certain things you should try before you die or else you will sit up on your deathbed crying: 'God, I wish I'd tried skiing, whistling with two fingers in my mouth, Turkish baths, scuba diving and eating an oyster!' Bricklaying is one of them.

During the time it took me to learn to lay bricks, that little corner of the garden expanded into a universe. Quite apart from buying and transporting the bricks and cement, reading do-it-yourself brick books, and getting all the tools (and I can tell you that even a small brick wall soaks up endless amounts of brick and cement, involving repeated visits to the shops), I became obsessed with brickwork. I could hardly pass a house, or another garden, without peering at the bricks to find out whether they were one or two courses thick, and if they had been built using Flemish bond, Basildon Bond, James Bond or whatever the styles were called. And every time I laid a brick myself, it was an achievement, a little conquest. I felt I was building a cathedral.

As soon as I had finished it, of course, it started shrinking from being a cathedral or universe to being a little garden wall. Six months later I had stopped staring at other people's walls and lost my emotional involvement in bricks. A year later I had forgotten building the thing.

Rebuilding a railway is just like that.

Nobody had ever rebuilt a railway in Britain before, not a standard gauge, passenger-carrying, steam-driven railway, so they didn't even have books to go to as I did when I faced my wall; they had a run-down length of track in the depths of Sussex. Railway preservation is, in my view, a total misnomer, because you don't in the long run preserve anything – you replace it. Sleepers, track, paint, boilers, axles, huts, signals – they all sooner or later have to be replaced, and every single sleeper, every single lick of paint, represents an effort or an act of love which, at the time, seemed the most important thing in the world to the person who was doing it, as you will know if you have ever rebuilt a railway, or put up a garden wall. The Bluebell Line is a huge achievement.

And then someone comes along and says that the Bluebell Railway is a line which goes from nowhere to nowhere in the middle of nowhere.

Unfortunately, that is also true. It is the only line of all the ones we visited where I could not imagine any local resident hopping on to get somewhere. The Keighley and Worth Valley Railway actually have a special, and well-used, discount for locals and I met holidaymakers using the West Somerset line to move down the coast. There is even a woman who lives out in the wilds near Levisham who uses the North Yorkshire Moors Railway to get into Pickering and sell her hand-made besoms. But I cannot think why anyone should get a sudden urge to go from Sheffield Park to Horsted Keynes, and leap on the railway to do it. Even if they did, they would be well advised to go by road, as Sheffield Park is really a stately home a little way from the station, and not a place at all, and Horsted Keynes, although a real place, is a mile or more from the station. The result of thirty years work on the Bluebell Railway is a gleaming, wonderful, atmospheric railway that goes from nowhere to nowhere.

This was not at all the original intention.

The original intention was to reopen the line from East Grinstead to Lewes, a meandering and little-used

35027
LIFE BEGINS
AT 40
40
DEC. 11
1948-1988

Nº 1618

country branch line, which British Rail closed down in 1956 and again in 1958. (They had to reopen it in 1957 when a sharp-eyed local realised that it needed a Parliamentary measure to close it, which British Rail had forgotten to get.) Four full-time students put together a project for keeping the line open using railcars as an economical vehicle, organised public meetings, bent British Rail's ears, etc. In the words of one history of the line:

> 'Feeling the need for experienced adult support (students were not 'adult' in 1959) they had approached a number of known railway enthusiasts in the area, one of whom was happy to chair the meeting. This was Bernard Holden ... who has been there as a senior member of the management ever since.'

This is not quite the way the 'students' remember it. Having tracked one down thirty years later, I got the feeling from him that they didn't really want 'adults' interfering at all, but that they were obliged to because, at their age, they were not yet legally entitled to be directors, trustees, partners, whatever.

'We put together a highly professional feasibility study for keeping the Lewes to East Grinstead traffic going,' he told me. 'Even British Rail were pretty impressed. But when the older people joined us, they really hijacked the whole thing from us and turned it into a little steam preserved line, which hadn't occurred to us at all. There was a man called Horace May who was pretty ruthless – I even seem to remember him having his eye on a nice house at Sheffield Park, where a retired railway couple were living, and sure enough a little while later they were moved out, and he moved in. But even though our plans got lost in what eventually happened, we learnt a hell of a lot about life and how the big world operates from the experience.'

I think the limited steam operation was probably the more realistic option. The line had known only thirty years of prosperity, from its opening in 1883 to the First World War, and it was unlikely to regain it as

Above: *A Bluebell driver enjoying his tea break.*

Left: *The Horsted Keynes station master and his staff pass the time while waiting for the Sheffield Park train.*

Opposite: *Southern 1618 working its way through the West Sussex countryside.*

being just another branch line. By chopping off the Lewes end and abandoning the East Grinstead end, the bit left in the middle could flourish as something quite different: a steam experience. Horace May might have been ruthless, but when he became general manager it was probably what was needed. When other railway revivalists came to him for advice, he would ask exactly where the railway in question was. If it was far away, he would give encouragement and advice. If it was less than fifty miles away, he would advise them that it was a hopeless case and urge them to give up.

For the first eight years people could only come to the Bluebell Railway for practical advice. The Bluebell line could not go anywhere to get it. It was not until 1968, with the advent of the Keighley and Worth Valley Railway, that any other bit of BR line was reclaimed for passenger running, after which they came thick and fast. But to begin with they had to make their own way and, like the building of a garden wall, it was an agonising, step-by-step process. To start with, they only had one station; British Rail would not let them come into Horsted Keynes, which was still in use on a branch line to Haywards Heath, so they had to construct a temporary station, Bluebell Halt, just outside. There were no facilities there to run round the engine from one end of the carriages to the other, but by law you cannot operate a train with an engine at the back, so for four years they had to have an engine *both* ends on every trip. When finally they gained access to Horsted Keynes, and started acquiring more engines, they needed more sheds, which meant more volunteers....

It was a long and arduous journey, anyway. It's hard to convey just how much work is involved, because when you think of a little old branch line being turned into a dinky little preserved steam line, you automatically assume the workload must be the same or less. If it didn't take much to run a small country line, what's the problem with a private line, five miles long. But it's a quite false picture. The Bluebell Railway carries thousands more passengers than the old line ever did, using far fewer full-time staff, because it's going through its heyday *now*. And whereas the old line had the back-up of the parent company to rely on, from admin to heavy engineering, the Bluebell has to contain *everything* in its five-mile length, from catering to carriage sheds, from ballasting to boiler mending. Do I hear the word 'infrastructure'? I think I do. The line houses no less than thirty steam engines, for heaven's sake, which is a lot more than they used to house in the old days. The national rail network of Peru has only eighty engines. It makes you think.

'Creature comforts have to be upgraded as well,' says Bernard Holden in his office at Sheffield Park. 'Children are used to nice white lavatories at school, so we found ourselves replacing the old black loo that we always made do with. We had some catering facilities in an old, temporary coach, but people demanded more than that, so in 1986 we built our new catering block. I believe it's the largest on any preserved line.'

Bernard Holden? Good heavens, this is the very same man who chaired that very first meeting all those years ago in 1959. A lot older now – well, thirty years older, to be precise – and slowing down a bit, but still in touch with everything that's happening, even if much of it is being done by a younger generation. I wondered if he had had previous railway experience before those four students had contacted him. Yes, with Southern Region, he says, but further afield as well.

'I worked for four years on the Bengal-Assam Railway, actually – well, I was seconded to it during the war. Curiously enough, there was a little girl growing up in the next valley who was later to become Michael Draper's wife, though of course I didn't know her then.'

He assumes I know who Michael Draper is. It's hard not to. He is the man in charge of the Severn Valley Railway, famous for his extrovert outspokenness. Quite a lot of private railways managers are known,

Opposite: *BR Standard class 2-6-4T loco No. 80064 bound for Horsted Keynes.*

but only Michael Draper is known to everyone.

'For quite some time, we soldiers running the Bengal-Assam Railway were the only British troops anywhere in the area, which was a sobering thought when a Japanese breakthrough was still on the cards. Running the railway was totally different from anything like Southern Region, where if you were a minute late you caused trouble. The Bengali staff couldn't care less if a train arrived on time or not. To be quite honest, they couldn't care less if the Japanese arrived or not.'

Rather more on his mind these days than the Bengal-Assam line is the Horsted Keynes – East Grinstead line. There isn't, of course, a line between Horsted Keynes and East Grinstead any more. That's why it's so much on his mind. There should be one. The longing of the Bluebell line to be reunited with East Grinstead, six miles away, is greater than West Somerset's longing for Taunton, the North Yorkshire Moors for Whitby or even the Dart Valley's for Totnes. They're just pining after old girl-friends. The Bluebell wants to reverse an amputation. And since 1975 they have been planning to get the missing line back, buying an old station here, a stretch of track there, thwarting a housing development at West Hoathly that would have dammed the line, even buying a whole railway bridge from North Wales that will replace one knocked down.... When you're a line that goes from nowhere to nowhere, your thirst for somewhere is very great.

As it is, the Bluebell is the only major preserved line with no stations in the middle. Not one. They tried creating one called Freshfield Halt, but no-body got on or off, so it lapsed. Nowhere to stand and await a passing train. Nowhere for me to get off with the bike and explore. That's probably why, in this last year, they have arranged a stop at a local farm where you can get off and step into a horse-drawn cart to be given an hour-long farm experience. That's all you can do, actually. You can't get off there and go somewhere. You can't get off and stand around, because you'll be whisked off on a compulsory farm experience. And

Above: *The Station Master giving his orders to a member of staff at Horsted Keynes.*

Above: *A sure-footed driver changes the white disk on Stroudley A1X class 0-6-0T No. 55* 'Stepney'.

Opposite: *Crowds turn out to see* Thomas the Tank Engine's *arrival at Sheffield Park.*

most extraordinary of all, you can't get off at the farm on the way up from Sheffield Park, although it's only a mile away – you have to wait until the return journey from Horsted Keynes before you can disembark at the farm. Very curious.

'I think it's something to do with the signalling,' says Bernard Holden vaguely. 'It's hard to signal a stop from this end. Something like that.'

During a long conversation with Bernard Holden, I never heard him mention Father Christmas once. But when I go and beard John Hill, general manager, in his office next door, Santa Claus crops up about every five minutes. Can a railway conversation be so obsessed with Yuletide? You bet it can. Santa Claus Specials are big money-spinners on the Bluebell Railway.

'They were first introduced by the Keighley and Worth Valley Railway,' says John admiringly, 'and they were a brilliant idea. Santa Claus ... some little presents ... perhaps a glass of something for the parents ... and suddenly you had packed trains at Christmas time, when before you didn't even have trains. A brilliant way to fill a blank month. They all love it, and we benefit from it.'

John Hill also likes taking his turn at being Father Christmas, that much is clear, though he says that distinguishing little children's genders these days is getting harder. He always makes a point of asking their names, to find out. But even the names are getting harder to classify by sex. Last year one child owned up to the name Galen.

'I still don't know if it was a boy or girl.'

John, from Merseyside, spent twenty years working on British Rail, though not very happily towards the end. He spent two years in retail management, not very happy, became redundant. He happened to be in London the day the Bluebell Railway advertised this job in the *Standard,* applied for it, got it and, as far as I can make out, has finally discovered himself in a job which really suits him. Not so much because of the railway context, but because there is a streak of the showman in him which has finally blossomed.

'Look, we've got to realise that we can no longer sell

35027
40
DEC 11

35027
35027
40

ourselves just as a steam railway. The novelty and thrill of visiting a steam railway is beginning to wear off, especially as more and more are opening up, and none is closing down. There are too *many* steam lines, probably, spreading the available knowledge and enthusiasm too thin, but that's by the by – don't want to get controversial. The point is that we aren't just a railway, we're a tourist attraction. We have to fight for people in the tourist market place, just like all the others, and that means thinking of new things to attract them with, new bits of publicity, new ways of getting in the paper. I read in the *Sun* one day that Rick Parfitt, with the group Status Quo, says his big ambition is to go on a steam train. What do you do? Say, Isn't that nice? No, you get on the phone to the *Sun* straightaway, as I did, tell them to get Rick down here with a photographer and we all got a nice feature out of it. It's cheekiness that gets you in the media, cheekiness that gets you in the money. I suppose it was cheekiness that made me write to Richard Branson, Paul Getty Jr, and others, telling them that they had to support the Bluebell line.'

Wow. Did he get any money?

'I didn't even get an answer. But that's not the point. You try everything and some of it comes off, some of it doesn't. It hasn't done too badly for us.'

He shows me a tourist board report on the ten most popular tourist attractions in Kent and Sussex, and the Bluebell is way up the list with over 200,000 passengers a year. Canterbury Cathedral is right out in front with over 2,000,000, though. I wonder if the Archbishop has the same sort of outlook as John Hill?

'This is a cathedral, of course, but it's more than just a cathedral. It's part of the leisure industry as well. Now, if we are to keep at the top of the league, we must keep innovating, and I've been dreaming up some ways in which we can incorporate Father Christmas this Christmas. I don't think we've had a grotto next to the crib before. Incidentally, has Richard Branson answered yet...?'

Perhaps not. But even if John Hill is a railway man through and through, his preoccupation with publicity is typical of a younger breed of railway manager. A famous name in the paper on a visit to the Bluebell can put figures up for months. Being featured in a film or television series can do the same, and it needs that sort of boost because although it seems to be near to London, if you're viewing it from Yorkshire or Somerset, it is (as I seem to have said) in the middle of nowhere. I have a *Collins Road Atlas* in the car. The Bluebell Railway is not even marked on it. Mark you, there's a man who hates railways at Collins, because the maps only mark BR stations, and not the lines joining them.

'We depend entirely on people who come by car – there is a bus service to us *one* month of the year. I suppose it's just too affluent round here for buses. It's certainly so affluent that when we were looking for help with the permanent way, we couldn't get a Manpower Services Commission scheme going. So, we had the bright idea of going to the probation service instead, and via them we got a really good gang of lads.'

John Hill doesn't, indeed, give up easily. But it occurs to me that there is one bright notion he hasn't tried yet, one which hasn't been tried by any railway, and which could make somebody's fortune. It came to me some time after I had listened to his satisfied list of visits they had had that year from film location units for *Campion*, *Portrait of a Marriage*, *Poirot* and other television things (also, apparently, from the Ann Summers sex set-up who were doing a saucy calendar shoot). Nothing startling about this. Every railway you go to likes to list *their* film visitors. But what struck me suddenly was that when people film at a preserved steam railway, they either want to do a period piece of fiction or an up-to-date documentary. It's either Sherlock Holmes or A Day Out on the Bluebell. Nothing else.

What you never get is a piece of *fiction* about a modern preserved steam railway. Not drama, perhaps; what I am inclined to favour would be a television situation comedy set in the world of steam preservation. All those film crews coming down the

Opposite: *A stray cow takes fright as loco No. 35027 charges by on its way to Horsted Keynes.*

Right: *Southern loco 1618 waiting for signals to change at Horsted Keynes station.*

Opposite: *Southern loco 1618 approaching Horsted Keynes through an avenue of trees near Freshfield Halt.*

whole time with actors in Edwardian costume pretending to be dead passengers, when staring them in the face is modern, real life material, throbbing with possibility.

For instance, there would be some mileage in inventing a railway which had two people in charge, one a founder-member who has seen the railway grown from the original acorn and is basically 'Wouldn't–railways–be–nice–if–it–weren't–for–the–people?' type, and the other a younger, go-ahead man who is avid for publicity of every kind. The conflict between the two (each of whom would sometimes be in the right) could be richly comical and instructive. Does it sound entirely based on Bernard Holden and John Hill? Well, it's not – for the older man I am actually thinking of a founder member of a quite different line who said to me one day that I really ought to pay a visit to the Talyllyn Railway, the earliest of them all, because 'they've still got railway preservation there as it used to be'.

Railway preservation as it used to be! He was in favour of railway preservation *preservation*, and didn't like the newer kind of preservation, with all its publicity and gimmickry. Then, one day, a gang of girls and photographers would arrive to do scenes for a sexy calendar at the railway ... or a famous rock musician arrives, with a team from the *Sun*, to take his first ride on a train.... There is any amount of conflict

Nº 1618

Opposite: *The station cat at Horsted Keynes has found a sure way of safe-guarding the luggage.*

available in a preserved steam line, between directors and workforce, workforce and volunteers, volunteers and enthusiasts who know everything except how to get their hands dirty, between people who like dressing up in guard's uniforms and clipping tickets and people who wouldn't be seen dead outside dirty dungarees. Years ago, I wanted to write a television sitcom set in a museum. My first wife worked in a museum and the tales she told me of the hatred, revenge, back-stabbing, politicking, betrayal, broken promises and sexual intrigue that go on in museums made my blood run cold. Steam railways are pretty nice by comparison. But not too nice.

A sitcom set in a steam railway would send attendance figures soaring and it might also provide a mainstream programme about steam that enthusiasts approved of. Generally, television steam programmes do *not* satisfy the insiders. At the Festiniog Railway, for instance, they told me not to bother seeing that half-hour programme that Wynford Vaughan Thomas had once made about the line, as most of it was about the village of Portmeirion, not about trains at all, for God's sake. I made a effort to see the film. The best ten minutes were set in Portmeirion, incorporating a fascinating interview with the aged Clough Williams-Ellis. The rest, about the line, I found fairly tedious and skimpy.

I remembered, by the way, to ask John Hill why the trains on the Bluebell Line didn't stop at the farm till the return journey – was it really to do with signalling?'

'Not at all. It's because it's quite a stiff gradient from here for a mile or two, 1 in 75, and if trains stop at the farm going, it'd be bloody difficult for them to start again.'

It's also a pretty stiff gradient up the road from Horsted Keynes station to Horsted Keynes the village, a mile of agonising bicycling. Nice pub there, the Green Man, plastered with many a photo of the old railway line, though God knows how many people make it up from the station to have a look. They don't do overnight accommodation, so I ended up in The Griffin, at nearby Fletching, and I couldn't have done better if I'd been staying with old friends – a wonderful village pub, with a creative restaurant incorporated and six bedrooms all with four-poster beds. In the morning I was awoken by the ringing of bells and battering on doors. I went to investigate, as nobody else wanted to. I found that the lady who had come to cook the breakfasts was locked out and she fell on my neck in sheer gratitude. While waiting for breakfast, I went outside on what was by then a soft, sunny summer morning and sat at one of the tables in the garden overlooking the highly salaried countryside of Sussex, tapping out an article for *The Independent*. This is the life, I thought. Then I looked up to see the breakfast lady tripping across the lawn with a tray of tea.

'Thought you might like this,' she dimpled.

This really is the life, I thought. And I am now trying to remember what led me to mention The Griffon in the first place – ah, yes, I remember. There were no pictures of trains on my walls, but there was an old black and white photograph of what looked like a large part of the British army going off to the Boer War. It turned out to be nothing of the kind, only the funeral of the Earl of Sheffield in 1909, who either was an important and rich man or had a lot of personal friends in the British army. He was important and rich, and was the leading spirit behind the building of the railway line from Lewes to East Grinstead in 1883 which now survives as the Bluebell Line. It seems that in 1884 or thereabouts his direct interest in railways ebbed, but his interest in Sheffield Park station was enormous as it contained a telegraph office, and he apparently delivered most of his voluminous and opinionated correspondence through it, keeping the clerk working almost exclusively for him. If it was still there today, it would have been patronised for an article in *The Independent*.

Failing which, there is always the railway to go on again, that wonderful trip from nowhere to nowhere through the most beautiful nowhere. There is the

DEPARTURES
LEWES

collection of thirty engines to see, and there are coaches galore to see, but I am not a coach or an engine man on a soft summer day, so I went on an expedition I can thoroughly recommend; a trip down the line which does not exist yet. There is something haunting and evocative about a line closed down and forgotten, like a ruined Gothic priory, but there cannot be anything much more mysterious than a closed down line which is threatened with re-opening. The canyon-like entrance to the echoing tunnel which goes right beneath the village of Sharpthorne, damp and dripping ('But all Sussex tunnels are wet', says Bernard Holden, making it sound like a bit of ancient wisdom). The enormous climbing castle in Sharpthorne playground which turns out not to be a child's structure at all, but a ventilation shaft to the tunnel. Kingscote Station, at present with no trains to serve and yet already spruced up and restored, like a bride waiting at the altar. Above all, the main obstacle to the reopening of the line, the sixty-foot cutting at Imberhorne which has patiently been filled in over the years with local authority rubbish until that huge hole in the ground has become a sleek, man-made mountain. Once, man cut out a huge notch in the hillside to let trains through. Then man thought better of it and filled it with rubbish. Now man wants to change his mind and put trains back. To remove the rubbish, he will have to dig another hole somewhere to put the rubbish in. The contents of that hole, the earth and rubble, will have to be stored somewhere else.

From the vantage point of another planet, man must sometimes look a bit confused, but from the parapet of the bridge that once looked down on echoing trains and now looks down on a false forest floor, the breathtaking ambition of the project makes up for everything. All railway lines in the steam preservation world are haunted by a glorious past, but the Bluebell Railway is also haunted by a glorious future, the ghost of things to come. At one end of the line the old Earl of Sheffield waving goodbye, at the other end the station-master of East Grinstead beckoning. In the middle, mountains to be made into molehills. But it can be done, as you will know if you have ever built a garden wall.

Opposite: *A bird's eye view – on the approach to Horsted Keynes.*

Right: *A guard gives the all clear signal at Horsted Keynes station.*

Below: *A pristine station is the result of compulsory cleaning duty for the staff.*

34092

5 The Line of the Film of the Book

The Keighley and Worth Valley Railway

Previous page: *British Railways built, Bulleid designed, West Country class 4-6-2, No. 34092,* 'City of Wells' *pulling out of Keighley.*

Opposite: *BR standard class 4 4-6-0 No. 75078 running through to Haworth.*

KEIGHLEY is a large town in Yorkshire which would be much better known if it were not overshadowed by the cities of Bradford and Leeds, scarcely a dozen miles away. Sixty thousand inhabitants are usually enough to make you stand out, but not when you've got Bradford and Leeds upstaging you. Even the Airedale Valley in which they all stand is more famous than Keighley, if only by having a dog named after it, and Ilkley, just across the valley on the north side, has acquired comparative fame by not being ashamed to feature in a song which must be among the top twenty sung when folk gather, get slightly drunk and want to sing slightly nonsensical songs. Nobody sings about Keighley.

Things didn't get much better in 1974 when the reorganisation of local government in Britain took away much of Keighley's independence, pride and historic status, and gave it to Bradford. I met one girl in Keighley who was now high up in local service, but had only been able to achieve promotion by accepting transfer first to Bradford, where she had attracted favourable attention from the hierarchy.

Below: *The traditional atmosphere of Oxenhope station.*

'If I'd stayed in Keighley all along,' she said, 'I would probably never have been noticed by the powers that be in Bradford. Well, it's not right, is it?'

No, it certainly isn't. But Keighley does have something that nobody else has for miles around. It has a steam railway. One hundred and sixty thousand people every year come to ride on the Keighley and Worth Valley Railway. I would be surprised if 160,000 people go to Ilkley to see Ilkley Moor and trace the source of 'Ilkley Moor bar t'at'. But, 160,000 people do turn up during the season – and beyond – to travel on the service which takes them up the Worth Valley, the valley which goes up south at right angles to Airedale, full of little mill towns, till it gets to Oxenhope and stops. The railway stops, that is; the valley goes on up till it looses itself on the moors, the lonely moors which go on and on until they drop down into Hebden Bridge.

'The Keighley and Worth Valley Railway?' said the man on the North Yorkshire Moors Railway, when I mentioned it to him. 'Aye, they have some good little stations there. Lovely stations.'

This was his way of saying that the line was not very long. (It was also his way of saying that nobody would visit the NYMR just to see the stations.) And it is true that however slowly you travel, and however many stations you stop at, it does not take very long to complete the five-mile journey to Oxenhope. But from the moment you walk down the long, echoing, wooden-floored and roofed-over entrance to the station, from the slightly bleak industrial scene outside, you find yourself in another world where nobody wants to go particularly far or fast, because it's so nice just going. The KWVR station at Keighley, with its hanging baskets of flowers, its slightly rustic but quite elaborate architecture, and its deep maroon and cream decor, manages to be both functional and picturesque at the same time. And to look a great deal more attractive than the British Rail station bang next door.

The KWVR people are very glad that the British Rail

Above: *Building up steam as the all clear is given for departure from Oakworth station.*

Opposite: 'City of Wells': *tender first past Ebor Mill.*

station is next door, because it gives them a lot of extra traffic. BR and the KWVR have struck up an understanding so that main line services connect up with steam line schedules, and just before the first steam of the day, there is usually a respectable small cascade of passengers pouring across the bridge from Keighley (BR) to Keighley (KWVR), which can be seen going into reverse at the end of the day's steaming. But the KWVR people must also be glad, though they don't say so, that the unsensational decor of their nationalised neighbours contrasts so strikingly with their own Homes and Stations colour scheme and their unashamedly old-fashioned atmosphere, their pleasantly fussy little collection of ticket barriers, tea stalls, shops and old posters.

I thought, in my innocence, that the maroon and cream – deep purple maroon on the bottom half of the elegant pillars and anything below shoulder height, cream aloft, reaching up into the roofwork – were the inspired choice of some tasteful director's wife. I should have known better. Colour schemes on railways, are all to do with the original livery, and it is a matter of chance whether you are struck with something as attractive as that, or something more lugubrious. And when the train arrives in the station, like actors bursting on to the stage, the maroon and cream of the carriages complete the theatrical setting.

In the first train I took out of Keighley I was surrounded by a father and six children. Not all his; four of them were Asian, two English like himself, and it gave my tired old liberal feelings a boost to see such an obviously happy and unconsciously integrated group. Especially as the night before, while sampling an amazing selection of real ales in a rough-and-ready Keighley pub called The Grinning Rat, I had eavesdropped on the sort of conversation I don't hear much near Bath, where I live. All about Muslim-only schools, and separate cultures, and it-didn't-seem-right somehow. 'All right, call me a racist,' said one tight-faced little man, in a tight suit and tight bow-tie, 'call me a racist if you like, but I wouldn't be against sending them home. I know what I'm talking about when it comes to race. I'm Jewish....' It didn't seem to strike him that if people were sent back to their origins, he wouldn't be there laying down the law in Yorkshire.

But a more significant traveller on that train was the young Japanese student, smiling and nodding in the middle of the Asian/English family. He could hardly speak English, but I managed to elicit from him the fact that part of his cultural tour of Europe was a pilgrimage up the railway to visit the Brontë stronghold of Haworth. He had read *Wuthering Heights* by Charlotte Brontë, and thought it a wonderful book, even in Japanese, and the Keighley and Worth Valley Railway must thank its lucky stars that the Brontës decided to settle bang on their line.

OAKWORTH
VENUS SOAP
OAKWORTH
75078

Among the usual railway publications on the station bookstall there are the complete works of the Brontë sisters ('A bloke from Australia bought five this morning,' the bookseller told me with satisfaction), a sign that the KWVR is well aware of the girl's pulling power.

The normal image of the Brontë lifestyle doesn't include railways. Rather, the common concept of the family is of a group of unhappy people stranded in a cheerless parsonage up on the moors, well away from industrial goings on. This mistaken image has actually stirred Juliet Barker, who was the curator of the Brontë Parsonage Museum until 1989, to begin work on a biography to put the picture straight, her complaint being that almost all Brontë biographies are written by literary people who concentrate on the gloom and doom. She, a historian, would far rather stress that they all had a comparatively happy life, lived longer than the average for the time and were well involved with the social goings on of the area.

And if a *railway* historian were to write about them, would he have anything to say? He would. Here is a biographical sketch of the Brontë family taken from a history of the railway written in 1962 by R.O.T. Povey, and a remarkable sketch it is too.

Above: *One of the many well-preserved gas lamps at Oxenhope station.*

Above: *The Damens station sign and original gas lamp painted in the Worth Valley Railway colours.*

Opposite: *Loco No. 75078 pulls into Oakworth station, location for the film of* The Railway Children.

'Any reference to Haworth would be incomplete without some reference to this famous family. Unfortunately, we must admit that they had no direct connection with the railway, because they had all died before the Prospectus was issued. (The Rev. Patrick Brontë, the last of the family, died in 1861, having been Rector of Haworth for over 40 years.) However, we do know that they were interested in railways, as the Rev. Patrick is shown as one of the Promoters of the Manchester, Hebden Bridge and Keighley Junction Railway previously mentioned. Ann, Emily and Charlotte invested part of the legacy which they received from their aunt in the York and North Midland Railway Company, whose chairman was the notorious George Hudson. In the 'Railway Times' for 17th September, 1845, appears a list of subscriptions to a testimonial fund for George Hudson, and the three sisters are listed as contributing £1 each.

'Shortly after this, however, Charlotte expressed grave doubts about the railways being a sound investment, but Emily prevailed upon them to leave their money where it was – with sad results.

'As for brother Branwell, he was appointed to a post on the Leeds and Manchester line at Sowerby Bridge station in October 1840. Early in 1841 he was transferred to Luddendenfoot and about a year later he was dismissed for gross irresponsibility.'

Quite apart from being the only account of the Brontës which does not mention that they ever wrote a book between them, it is very brave of Povey to admit that their experience of railways was uniformly disastrous, though he might have added that Branwell's offence was to be in charge of a booking office while very drunk. The only advantage that ever accured to the Brontës from railways came after they were all dead, and Haworth (which, by the way, is to all intents and purposes pronounced Howarth) had its own railway station. Povey, though, is right to stress the industrial encroachment of the Worth Valley, without which there would be no line at all.

They are grand little stations alright, but that is not why they were built – the line was fought for and won because the worsted mills that spangled the valley needed to get coal as quickly and cheaply as possible, and to ship out their produce in the same way. Rail was the answer, or at least a much more modern and efficient answer than the horses and carts which struggled up and down the valley. The mill-owners had the money, influence and Wesleyan persistance to get things moving, and although it took five years from the granting of Parliamentary assent in 1862 to build the line (a mile a year!), it duly opened with the customary bands and dinner, and equally traditional breakdown of the train on launching day. One of the most unexpected snags in the building of the line had been the digging of a tunnel in Keighley under a large Wesleyan chapel which had contrived to crack the chapel's fabric badly enough to make it unsafe for

worship. For once, though, many of the people behind the railway were also trustees of the chapel, and as the railway could not be rerouted, the chapel was taken down and rebuilt elsewhere.

It was exactly one hundred years from Parliament giving the line the nod to British Rail deciding to close it down, and it took even longer than five years for the newly formed Preservation Society to reopen it. Apart from the recently reopened Bluebell Line way down south, there was no precedent in England for a successfully rescued line and it's hard to imagine now the courage needed by the original members to stick to their vision of their own line in the face of doubt, and more especially in the face of the quite extraordinary slowness of British Rail solicitors to agree to a contract of sale, which was leisurely even by the standards of solicitors.

The line was born to carry profitable freight. By the time it was reborn, the freight had vanished or was going by road, and such of the mills as remained open were often being used for another kind of sweated labour: battery chickens. But in 1968 there was a new kind of industry to mine, tourism, and an inroad into this goldmine was provided by an extreme piece of luck, the filming of *The Railway Children* on the Keighley and Worth Valley Railway. The line provided exactly the mixture of stone cottages, green fields, industrial backdrop and hint of moorlands needed by the story, and for seven weeks engines were repainted and stations smartened up and the years rolled back to recreate the Edwardian setting of the only film which has ever received its world premiere in Keighley.

It was a smash hit then, and it is a children's classic today; for many modern children it is probably the only sharp contact with steam – along with Thomas the Tank Engine – that they get. In 1989 there was a

Left: *BR Standard loco 75078 all steamed up and ready to go with* 'City of Wells' *outside Haworth loco shed.*

Right: *Admiring crowds gather to see* 'City of Wells' *at Oxenhope station.*

34092

Above: *The hanging baskets and elaborate architecture of Keighley station.*

stage production of *The Railway Children* at the York Theatre Royal, and to whip up a bit of publicity local television brought the cast across to the KWVR for a nostalgic ride up the line. Significantly, for all the 'children' in the cast, it was their first ever ride on a steam train. A week later, BBC showed a half-hour film featuring the actor Bernard Cribbins returning after over twenty years to the scene of the filming of *The Railway Children* to indulge in another bout of nostalgia. It wasn't quite clear from the film just how nostalgic Cribbins was (his part in filming the role of Mr Perks, station porter at Oakworth, seems to have taken not much more than a fortnight), but *The Railway Children* was certainly a glorious moment for Graham Mitchell.

'I happened to be the rostered guard on the train in the week of the filming,' says Mitchell, who is now chairman of the preservation society, 'and the director, Lionel Jeffries, asked to see how I would wave the train off from Oakworth. Well, in fact I would only lift my flag, but I went over the top and did a dramatic flourish, which he liked well enough to keep in the film. "Take it away, Mr Mitchell", cried Bernard Cribbins, and I cried back, "Thank you, Mr Perks", flourished my flag and climbed in the train.'

This single speaking line in major motion pictures has still not led to any further offers to Mr Mitchell, but the film worked a miracle for the line. The year after the film came out the attendance doubled from 60,000 to near 130,000 and has never slipped back even when the novelty of the film had worn off. It's a remarkable thought, but despite the presence of the Brontës (and I can't think of any line which has such lucrative literary ghosts), the filming of *The Railway Children* was a much more important cultural event for the line. Indeed, the Cribbins programme proves that the filming now has its own inbuilt nostalgia; nostalgia for a piece of nostalgia, as it were. Jusc how far nostalgia and the media are entangled is proved by the beckoning publicity for a museum in Haworth called Bygone Days. 'Come and see the actual historical items used in many famous television productions!' it says.

By good luck, Graham Mitchell was also the rostered guard on several trains on which I passed up and down the valley, and enthusiastically pointed left and right at features I should not miss. Dark-whiskered in the film, grey-bearded now, he still has a bubbling eagerness which you might think would be dimned after so many years of preservation. Ingrow Station, which is actually a station from Lancashire which we brought brick by brick and has just been opened by Lord Ingrow ... that's the building over there we aim to turn into a showcase for historic coaches, road vehicles, that is .... there's Damens Station, the smallest in Britain, blink and you miss it (I blinked, and I missed it) ... here's Oakworth Station, still kept as it was in Edwardian or Railway Children days.... It's all gas lighting still, you know. It's got fifty-nine working gas lights. Oakworth Station is actually the third largest gas lighting establishment in the country, after the Royal Parks, and somewhere in Sheffield.

Opposite: *The upkeep of stations such as Damens is entirely dependant on volunteers.*

WAY OUT
PLEASE SHOW TICKETS
2

34092

'And here we are in Haworth,' he said, gazing out at the holiday throng. 'Sometimes I rub my eyes when I see so many people on one of our little stations. Where do they all *come* from? I wonder. And do they realise they're allowing me to pursue such a magnificent hobby?'

At Oxenhope, the glittering little station at the end of the line, he gives me a tour of the coach shed and I ask him where he gets new carriages from.

'Generally we get them from British Rail, who put them out to tender to all the steam lines, when they no longer need them.'

'I suppose you preserved steam lines get together and fix it between you? You know, I'll this one, you take that one?'

'Like hell we do! We private lines are friends on the surface, but...'

One aspect of their rivalry seems to be in the choosing of a slogan. Sometimes they stick to a carefully worded claim such as the West Somerset Railways's 'Britain's Longest Preserved Railway' or the Festiniog Railway's painstaking 'The Oldest Passenger-Carrying Narrow-Gauge Railway in Britain'. But there is some conflict, surely, between the Severn Valley Railway's 'Britain's Premiere Steam Railway', the Dart Valley's 'Supreme in Steam' and the KWVR claim to be 'Britain's Finest Independent Railway'. Could they *all* be the finest?

'Well, now,' says Mr Mitchell, cleverly keeping off the ropes, 'what I would say is that we have three outstanding claims. This first is that we are a complete branch line, working out of a main line station and providing the only real complete experience of what a branch line used to be, with all the feeling of country and town mixed – and I may say that at weekends we do get a lot of local passenger traffic, who all get a healthy resident's discount. And I think we are the only line that operates all the year round, even if it is weekends only in winter.

'Secondly, we have a relationship with a main line station that no other line quite has, totally integrated. BR have really become quite co-operative over the years, and the local Metro service much more so.

Above: *An exchange of tokens at the Damens signal box.*

'Thirdly, uniquely, we are entirely run by volunteers. Well, we have one full-time, paid girl on the switchboard, but apart from that we have *always* depended on non-paid volunteers, which no other line ever has, and I think this creates a wonderful esprit de corps. We don't even have a general manager. The most we have is an R.O., a Responsible Officer who is in charge for the day, who might be any of four or five senior figures. Today, it's me.'

Which was why, a few moments later, having spotted a small lineside fire just outside Oxenhope, he was off to deal with it, or rather, to get someone to deal with it. It was significant, by the way, that he used the word 'volunteer' and not 'enthusiast'. A notice put up in 1989 in several stations helps to explain why.

Notice to Visitors, Enthusiasts and Photographers.
Following some complaints by local residents of trespass and damage allegedly caused by visitors; visitors are urged and requested to refrain from

Opposite: 'City of Wells' *storming out of Keighley station.*

Opposite: *Hammering through the Haworth Moors, 75078 approaches Oxenhope.*

anything which could give rise to complaint, such as trespassing on the line, lineside or farmland areas, unless they have permission, in particular climbing signals, telegraph poles or walls.

January 1989.

Volunteers are the unsung, unnamed heroes who do the back-breaking work of actually building a line and giving the engine major surgery. As Mike Goodall says in his 1983 history, *Worth Valley Revival,* the KWVR is now virtually a new line, because everything has been replaced since BR days, and lifting 1,000 rails, each weighing two and a half tons, is some feat.

Enthusiasts are the chaps with encyclopaedic knowledge, video cameras and bulging notebooks, who scramble around the countryside breaking branches and fences to get a good shot. They are the ones who write in indignantly when a railway paints a coach in what they consider to the the wrong livery, and who went almost mad when the KWVR allowed an engine to be entirely *wallpapered* for a wallpaper commercial. Volunteers, being nice, diplomatic people, usually let them get on with it, but I think an outsider like me is allowed to echo their unspoken feeling that enthusiasts get more out of steam than they put into it. (As the man at Bewdley Station on the Severn Valley Railway who had been restoring a tank engine for eleven years said to me: 'It would be nice if some of the people who photograph the engine also put a few bob in the contribution tin.')

What both volunteers and enthusiasts have in common, I suppose, is that they are all slightly mad to be doing this; it's just that the madness takes different forms, sometimes as an urge to get your hands dirty, sometimes as an urge to collect and document. In John's case, it was combined with an urge to follow Fulham Rugby League Club. Until a few years ago John lived in Slough with a job, a passion for railways and this thing about Fulham. When the surge in house prices came along, he worked out that he could sell his house in Slough, buy one much cheaper in Yorkshire and use the profit to support himself frugally while he did what he really wanted to do in life: be a guard on the KWVR and see Fulham playing up north.

'I did go and have a look at the North Yorkshire Moors Railway,' said John, 'but it was too remote for me to consider going to become a guard there.'

Remote from what? Civilisation? Slough?

'No, from the main Rugby League centres.'

Most of us would only dream about doing a thing like that, but John actually did it, and I think he was about the happiest guard I met. He stressed to me that being a guard is not a soft option, even on a small steam line. The training is long, the examination is thorough and the failure rate is high. Every guard I talked to stressed this. They might also have stressed the medical side of it, because Sam was never allowed to become a guard or driver on account of something suspect to do with his lungs.

I met Sam Jennings on Oakworth Station during one of those timeless gaps (an hour? a day? a year?) between trains, when stations go to sleep and you can hear the birds again. Sam is a bronze-pated, well-

Below: *Along the platform at Damens – the smallest station in Britain.*

75078
BUFFET

34092

seasoned 72-year-old, who is in charge of the station for the day along with Roy and who had come into volunteering in a most unusual way.

'I was in property in Wakefield, with no particular interest in trains, and I met the Bishop of Wakefield at Rotary. Well, of course, the Bishop of Wakefield was the well-known Railway Bishop, Eric Treacy, and he was drumming up support for the Keighley and Worth Valley Railway and he said to me, Why not become a member? Why not? I said, and I did, and didn't think much more about it. A bit later he came to me and said, Why not come out on the footplate for a day? And I thought, Why not? and I did, and I was hooked for life.'

The extraordinary thing to my mind is not that Sam should have come to steam trains via a bishop (there is a well attested network between church and railways) but that he should have come so late in life, without either a railway background or a history of previous addiction – railway enthusiasm almost always has its roots in the early days. Once there, though, and once barred from working on the trains by his lungs, he made up for lost time by getting Oakworth Station in shape.

'It was a mess,' said Roy suddenly, who didn't say much. 'The weeds had grown like a jungle. Everything was growing everywhere.' He fell silent again.

'I knew quite a lot about gardening,' said Sam, 'so I took over replanting the station. My father taught me all about gardening by a very good system. What happened was that he gave us each a small plot of land and told us how to grow things, and then if we ever grew anything which was used by our mother in the kitchen, like a lettuce or a cabbage, we actually got paid for it. That gives you some incentive, I can tell you. So I got to work not just doing the flowerbeds and flower baskets, but planting that hedge over there.'

That hedge over there wasn't a hedge; it was more like a grove. If you sit on Oakworth Station, on one platform, and stare across the line at where you expect the other platform to be, you find yourself looking at a thick deciduous curtain twenty or thirty feet high, full of hawthorn, silver birch and mountain ash. They were all eighteen-inch seedlings when Sam put them in.

'It wasn't so much to make the place look pretty,' said Sam, 'more because there was a terrible eyesore behind, some kind of private zoo which was a real mess. Remember that Roy?'

'Real mess,' said Roy. 'So bad they came round and told the man to close it down.'

'But even without the zoo there was a caravan site, and then there were houses, and it wasn't a lovely view, so all in all this screen of trees has been a great improvement.'

There is a sense, it has to be said, that a lot of railway people do screen themselves off from their environment. If it's not railway, they tend not to notice. Oakworth Station is a famous little station, both for the Railway Children connotations and for the fact that it has been preserved deliberately, almost doll's house-like, in an Edwardian bubble with the gas lighting and the deliberate policy *not* to sell anything on the premises, whether it's ice-creams or books and videos. (Most railway people wouldn't regret the ice-creams, but not to have a vast store of railway books and videos on tap goes against the grain.) But I had never heard anyone mention Oakworth the *place*, the little town that Oakworth Station was meant to serve, so I went to have a little wander round before I came down the steep lane to the station. It looked quite posh and green. I asked Roy and Sam about Oakworth.

There was a long silence.

It transpired that neither Sam nor Roy could even visualise what Oakworth looked like.

'I've been to this station thousands of times,' said Roy, 'but damned if I can remember ever looking at Oakworth.'

Mark you, the KWVR makes a better stab than most at integrating with the local community – no other steam line, I think, offers 50 per cent discount on travel to residents – and they were the first ever line to put

Opposite: 'City of Wells' *ready to leave Keighley station.*

75078

forward the idea which has made so much money for lines everywhere: the Santa Special. At a time of year when all tourists are hibernating and people don't go on trains for fun, someone had the brilliant idea of mounting Christmas Specials, with Santa Claus, presents and mince pies, and getting people out in their hundreds.

'I got involved with the very first one of all,' said Roy. 'Hadn't meant too. I was just coming off from changing batteries on a coach, and I was yelled at to come and help. Short-handed, as usual. All I was wearing was filthy overalls, so they stuck a driver's hat on me, stood me at the door of a coach and told me to take their money. It didn't occur to them that some of the people might not have the correct money – I spent most of my time screaming for change. What a mess. What a business. We were all bloody amateurs then. Not like now.'

'It's hard work being Father Christmas whether you're professional or amateur,' said Sam. 'Never a time for a pee or a bite, and hard at it all day fighting off the children who can wear you down so quickly. I was never a full-time Father Christmas, but I did my stint as substitute. The way it worked was that I would be waiting on Oakworth Station, all dressed up as Santa Claus, hiding indoors, and the train would stop and let off the real Father Christmas. He would wave to the train and pop through the door, and I would come straight out again and take over the train for half an hour while he had a bite to eat and a drink, and nobody ever suspected that I wasn't the same one. Then we'd swap back after he'd had a pee, which was no mean feat in those uniforms.'

Sam Jennings incidentally, was filmed shovelling coal for *The Railway Children*. He quite enjoyed it, it didn't make the final film. You could sit at Oakworth Station for hours just listening to the easy flow of the unassuming reminiscence, and it was while I was sitting there that I stumbled on one of the big secrets of the KWVR. Looking up and down the line for signs of trains, I realised you couldn't see very far in either direction. Well, I thought, come to that there isn't really any place on the line where you *can* see far in any direction; you're always waiting to see what's round the next corner. You've always got a wide view to the side, up the hills, into the mill towns, but never ahead where everything comes as a surprise. And *this* is what makes the line seem much longer than it really is; close-packed variety and lack of a far horizon.

Above: *Oakworth station – still kept as it was in Edwardian days.*

The reason that it has tight curves, and seems longer than it is, is that it is built in a valley bottom, following the curves of the river, which means also that it tends to miss the towns, usually perched safely above. Visitors to Haworth tend to blink when they get out of the station, as there is no sign of Brontë country anywhere. Not surprisingly; Haworth Station was in open country when it was first built and the real Brontë village is still several hundred yards further up the hill, towards the edge of the moors, preserved like a toffee apple beneath a gleaming layer of conservation, and marketing.

You might get the impression, too, that the KWVR has reached its final state of development, ticking over

Opposite: *BR Standard class 75078 on its laboured climb up the 1 in 60 gradient between Damens and Oakworth.*

QUINLAN BROS. LTD. · WALK MILLS
HAULAGE & STORAGE
34092

nicely with nothing left to achieve. It's certainly true that it can go no further – it doesn't have the territorial ambitions of the North Yorkshire Moors Railway, The West Somerset or the Bluebell. It starts one end at a main line station and ends at Oxenhope where only a four-mile tunnel could take it further. Those five miles are the beginning and end of the line. Yet Graham Mitchell sees this as an advantage,

'I've often noticed that when other lines make a special push to achieve a new target – getting into Kidderminster, perhaps – the ordinary services may suffer for a while. No point lengthening a line if the running of the line itself is going to suffer. But here at the KWVR we've always had specific improvements on the line itself to aim at – rebuilding Ingrow Station, putting locos on display to the public, all that sort of thing. Ahead of us we have the coach museum at Ingrow, better catering facilities, and my own special baby – the turntable at Keighley. People don't ride on steam lines for the sake of it as much as they used to, so you've got to expand the attractions, though always, as far as I'm concerned, in a railway-related way.'

Left: 'City of Wells' *forging its way out of Keighley's industrial landscape.*

By which he means, I suppose, that he wouldn't welcome a butterfly farm as at Buckfastleigh Station or an adventure playground as I heard suggested on the Bluebell Line at Horsted Keynes. But they've got so much here already it doesn't really matter; down to a trolley on Oakworth Station designed to take coffins.

'When I'm giving a party of schoolchildren a short talk,' says Sam Jennings, 'I always make a special point of showing them that.'

To underline the fraility of life, nearness of death, etc?

Good Lord, no. To emphasise that once upon a time the railway was the common carrier and, by law, *had* to take everything it was asked to take. Because in most cases it was the only way of taking things anywhere, including the body of your loved one back to his home. 'You see, children of today simply have no conception of what a huge part the railway played in everyone's lives. They simply have no idea.'

He didn't sound depressed at the thought. It must be hard to be depressed when you're working on the old KWVR.

6 Taking the Biscuit

The North Yorkshire Moors Railway

Previous page: *The ex-Southern class S15 4-6-0 No. 841* 'Greene King' *working its way north to Grosmont through the glacial gorge of Newtondale.*

Opposite: *BR class 4MT 2-6-4T No. 80135 crossing the River Esk in the Esk Valley on its way to Pickering.*

BEFORE I visited the North Yorkshire Moors my last port of call was the Keighley and Worth Valley Railway.

'You're going *where?*' they said. 'Oh, come on, stay here a bit longer.'

No railway can seriously believe you'd rather be somewhere else. I stayed another day and finally left.

'Well, if you *must* go,' they said, 'don't forget to ask the North Yorkshire Moors lot one question: why do they change managers so often?'

It sounded a loaded question to me, though it might just have been Keighley's way of boasting that they don't have a general manager and claim you don't need one. I could visualise the embarrassing scene at the NYMR.

'Any questions you'd like to ask us, Mr Kington?'

'Yes, actually. Why do you get through so many managers?'

'Ah ha! When a man asks that, it means he's been got at by the Keighley mob.'

I decided to keep the question in reserve, just in case. However, when I arrived at Pickering, I bought the latest edition of *Moors Line,* the NYMR magazine, and there on page one was the startling add:-

> NYMR General Manager required.
> We need an energetic person with managerial experience and financial acumen to develop further this major tourist attraction in North Yorkshire. Previous railway experience is desirable but not essential.'

I realised that the question would seem pretty tactless at the moment, as they changed managers yet again, and made a mental note to withdraw it.

I decided to apply for the job instead.

After all, I had the perfect cover. Here I was, apparently doing research on a book about steam railways, able to poke my nose in anywhere, and all the time doing groundwork on my application for the job of manager. I could worry about the managerial qualities and financial acumen later. And I had more railway experience than, well, Robert Reid, the new head of BR moving over from Shell UK. No problem.

It would be one up on the Keighley lot, too, if I got the job.

To set the scene, it is worth remembering that not all of Yorkshire is bumpy and rocky, up hill and down dale. All around the city of York there are flat plains spreading in each direction, and if you go north-east from York across the flat land (which undulates a bit near Castle Howard) you will eventually hit the North Yorkshire Moors, a rugged stretch of uplands dropping into the sea at inaccessible Whitby. Pickering is the last town you meet before you leave the flat country and go up into the hills, so you can imagine that as York was the big railway city round there, it was inevitable that if the railway came to Pickering, it would come the easy way from York.

Nothing of the sort happened. It came instead the hardest way possible, across the moors from Whitby. Pickering wasn't very important as a passenger town, but it had important lime quarries and the industrial demand was all up in the hills or over in the Esk Valley, not down at York. So, in 1836 the line across the moors was opened, built by George Stephenson, with trains being pulled by horse, just like on the Festiniog Railway which opened the very same year. One part of the line was too hard even for horses, in fact, the very steep part which comes down from Goathland to Grosmont. In the early days trains were hauled up here on a steel rope by a steam-operated winch; tremendous crashes took place whenever a rope parted. I did briefly consider reinstating this system when I became manager of the line, as it would obviously be highly exciting, with an element of risk, and I don't think passengers are hauled anywhere else in Britain in a truck up a steep incline, but I eventually decided against it on the grounds that steam fans would grumble too much at having to leave the train.

When they built the line they took the easiest route, up the river valley from Pickering back into the hills until they reached the watershed, then down the

stream bed the other side until they came to Grosmont and the Esk Valley – a sharp turn right there, and down to Whitby. The result of this is a curious one, that although the word Moors has overtone of uplands, exposed tops and miles and miles of heather and moorland, the railway never really rises out of a valley and thus even at the top is tucked away down between two ramparts, never getting the views you get on the Settle-Carlisle Line or the Festiniog. What you get instead though is just as grand in its own way. I considered briefly rerouting the line across the hilltops for a better view, but decided against it immediately on the grounds that George Stephenson almost certainly knew what he was doing.

In 1847 they switched from horses to steam. In 1865 they cut out that awkward steam-winched bit by building a new stretch of line from Goathland down to Grosmont. To celebrate the centenary of that improvement, British Rail closed the line down in 1965. Or at least they closed it between Pickering and Grosmont – the remaining half dozen miles to Whitby were part of the Esk Valley line, which wasn't closed though it was always under threat. So when the North Yorkshire Moors Railway Society, formed to reopen it, came charging over the skyline and, after eight years hard work, restarted the line in 1973, what they had was twenty miles of lonely moorland track.

By private lines standards, that is pretty long, longer than all but the West Somerset. They also have an ascent of 1 in 49 from Grosmont to Goathland which is pretty steep, one of the steepest anywhere in Britain. Now, a long line is good in that it attracts visitors who think they are getting value for money, as indeed they are, but a long line is also bad because – yes, anybody?

Please, sir, because it takes twice as long to run trains from one end to the other.

Very good. And why is that bad?

Because it's that much harder to step up the frequency of trains on the line.

But if you have enough trains, why can't you just send them out when you need them?

Above: *GWR 0-6-2T No. 6619 taking water at Pickering station.*

Above: *The station pub sign at Grosmont.*

Opposite *No. 80135 runs through the Goathland Moors towards Pickering.*

Because the NYMR is a single track railway, and there are only two passing places for trains coming the other way, at Goathland and at Levisham.

Well, instead of having more frequent trains, couldn't you have longer trains with more carriages?

Yes, but then you'll have to build longer platforms *and* you'll have to build a long loop line at Grosmont so that the engine can run round to the other end *and* you'll have to make sure you've got an engine which can pull the train up that wicked incline to Goathland....

It's dialogues like this which run through the minds of people who are preparing to apply for the job of railway manager. Mark you, all this is past history, these are problems which are largely overcome, or at least temporarily assuaged, but as Brian Cooke sagely writes in another part of the same *Moors Line* magazine, one of the railway's biggest problems is that 'it can offer to the public no major attraction other than riding on trains.' You will find a butterfly farm on the Dart Valley Railway, two station pubs on the Severn Valley, museums scattered here and there on all lines, and at the Bluebell Railway there is an ad:

> For that larger occasion we can arrange to erect marquees in our attractive grounds at Horsted Keynes amidst the glorious Sussex Wealden countryside.
>
> Fine barbeque or finger buffet menus available for up to 400 people.
>
> Bluebell Railway Catering, 082572-2008.

But on the North Yorkshire Moors Railway there is no attraction other than riding in trains. And that means that the biggest danger to a line like the NYMR is – yes, anybody?

Bad weather, sir?

No, nice try, but not really. People come in the summer even if the weather is not too hot. In fact, they tend to come *more* when the weather is dull, because then they say: Oh, it's not nice enough to go to the beach, let's go on an expedition. To us, hopefully.

Fire, sir?

Above: *The guard gives the all clear to the driver at Newtondale Halt.*

Fire? Oh, you mean, fire caused by sparks from the engine? Yes, bit of a problem this one, especially in a dry, hot summer like 1989. Unfortunately, there was one bad fire this year which spread right across from the line eastward to Fylingdales, where those three huge golf balls in the sky form our early warning system against sudden attack.

Did they spot attack by fire from the North Yorkshire Moors Railway, sir?

No, they don't face that way. We could easily have wiped them out. Luckily, the main A169 road acted as a firebreak and stopped the fire in time. Then for a long while we had to run diesels over the most fire-happy parts of the line in 1989, which as you can imagine was a real drag. But no, the real hazard to the NYMR is ... is ...

Success, sir?

Very good! Yes, success is the real danger. The more people you get on a line like this, the more over-crowded the trains become, the more pressure there is to run longer trains. Which means more powerful engines. And if the line doesn't own them, you have to hire them in. And then you find the accommodation is lamentable. Or, as Brian Cooke says:

> At present hire agreement locomotives have to either wait for small allotted amounts of spare time in the railway workshops, or their owners have to work outside in the yard whilst undertaking restoration and maintenance. Their locomotives, worth between £50,000 and £150,000 each, have to stand all year out in the open.

The solution, it seems, is to build a combination museum and workshop in the newly acquired field next door, in the hope that the entrance charge will pay for their construction. I do not know. I do not yet have the managerial experience and financial acumen. But I tell you one thing. Seeing yourself as management material makes you see steam railways in a quite different light. On all the other railways in this book I blithely skipped around as a visitor, but here I can see the bigger problems, and share in the dilemmas.

A bit depressing, really.

I think I'll just go for a train ride.

In the high season there are seven departures from Pickering every day, all steam-hauled and if you catch the first one you notice that the carriages are pretty spotless. You notice two cleaning ladies getting off, one of them with a fag dangling from her mouth. (Why is it that spotless cleaning ladies so often sport dangling cigarettes?) You compliment them on the spick and spanness of the coaches.

'It's all right if you're going from this end,' sniffs one of them. 'You should see the carriages coming from Grosmont. Not what I'd call a tiptop cleaning at all.'

Ah ha! So there is rivalry between Pickering and Grosmont, is there? This fits in with the pattern of every railway I have seen, rivalry between ends, rivalry between stations, even (on the Dart Valley

Opposite: *No. 6619 leaving the sheds at Grosmont.*

6619

SHOP
C1
80135

Railway) rivalry between two lines. I am all in favour, When I am manager of the NYMR, I shall encourage cleaning rivalry. Then we shall achieve final spick and spanness from both ends.

I realise that I am thinking like a manager again.

The departure from Pickering is undramatic, considering we won't be seeing another house for twenty miles, or not many. Pickering is rather a handsome little Yorkshire town, complete with ancient castle and more than one pub in the good pub guides, but you don't see much of that on your departure by rail. Indeed, you don't see much of anything until you have cleared a gaggle of empty carriages, some of them already set up for dinner. If there is anything that rivals the Santa Claus Specials as money-earners on the lines in this book, it is the Dining Specials or even Sunday Luncheon Specials, which offer a three-course meal and a there-and-back trip combined. Increasingly, the trains are being given names to make them sound special, like the Quantock Belle, Starlight Special, Severn Valley Limited or, here, the North Yorkshireman. Every time I have wandered into an admin area on any private line, there is always someone on the phone there saying: 'Yes, Saturday's menu does contain a vegetarian dish' or, more likely, 'I'm afraid we are totally booked now until November.' The idea obviously appeal. A six-month waiting list is not uncommon. On the West Somerset Railway, I remember, they had a list of hopefuls waiting for cancellations actually longer than the list of reservations itself. They would all love to put more of these specials on, but they are already stretching volunteer capacity to the limit.

On the shorter lines, like the Bluebell and Keighley, you have to steam *twice* up and down the line during dinner, but nobody seems to mind the incongruity. I once had a chat with the man who ran Westminster

Left: *A view from the hills round Goathland station as No. 80135 stops for passengers.*

Right: 'Greene King' *coming out of Newtondale Gorge into Levisham station.*

80135

Pier in London, from which many tour boats set off, and he told me that a captain of his acquaintance had taken the management of the Playboy Club and their intimates for an evening river cruise.

'Bit of a party it was,' he said, 'with lots of money and lots of blondes, and blue films, and adult entertainment, know what I mean? Anyway, they ordered the captain to lower all blinds, curtains etc., and the captain thought to himself: I'm not missing this! So he moored to the bank 400 yards down the river, left the engines running, went down to join in the party and took them 400 yards back three hours later, and not a bleeding soul noticed they hadn't been anywhere!'

A likely story. Good one, though. Just outside Pickering we pass a newly installed trout farm, where you can go and sit fishing. It would not be my idea of solitude to sit round an artificial pond with fishing rods, but I have noticed that anglers have the gift of instant loneliness. On the canal near Bath, where I live, the boat people, walkers and cyclists are a cheery lot, always nodding and waving, but not one fisherman has ever acknowledged the presence of anyone else's presence, sunk as he is in a mournful contemplation of eternity, like a prisoner in solitary. They also smoke a lot, like lady cleaners. The main pond at Pickering has an island in the middle. In the middle of the island there is a red phone box. I do not understand this, but perhaps it is there in case an angler should want to reach the Samaritans.

After the final glimpse of Pickering has disappeared, it's away up a twisting wooded valley where obvious signs of man get fewer and fewer, and the signs of encroaching wilderness gradually increase. The railway publishes an enterprising guide for eighty pence on what to see from the train, but it is sometimes hard pushed to find much and tends to fall back on things that used to be there, though I wished it offered an explanation of the mark on the wall, somewhat above human height, clearly labelled 'Les's Leap'. Who was Les and why did he leap in this lonely part of the woods?

The last time I came down this stretch was in 1986 for the television series, when we wanted to trace the history of increasing main line speed and managed to persuade the National Railway Museum at York to lend us a Sterling single-wheeler, a beautiful late Victorian engine with pair of huge driving wheels as big as a man. I think what persuaded them was money. The net result was that I found myself privileged to take a footplate ride on this high-stepping Victorian lady together with John Bellwood, a legendary expert in those parts, who shouted a bit of history for the film and looked only slightly bemused when water suddenly shot out of the firebox and across the cabin floor to drown our feet.

I can't remember what particular shattered pipe had caused this wound, which looked like a bad haemorrhage to me, but which they assured me was no worse than a nosebleed. The upshot was that we had to replan the shooting for another day, a great disappointment to the few railway enthusiasts who had learnt on the grapevine that this wholly unannounced, unscheduled outing was taking place and had turned up with their lineside videos, as if no movement by steam should ever go unrecorded. Indeed a few days later, on the totally unknown, rescheduled repeat shoot, there was one man sitting in a field with his camera, patiently waiting. It's a long and lonely wait up there if you've got the wrong day.

I am always strangely moved by the final run in to the first station on the line, Levisham. The valley suddenly broadens a bit and straightens out, allowing the track to run dead straight for a mile or so, perhaps the longest straight on any private steam line and certainly one place where you can look ahead and recapture the illusion of the old steam expresses charging for hour after hour across Britain. If the drivers ever open up to just above the speed limit, this is where it would be, and who could resist it occasionally? Who would ever know? What adds to the increasing feeling of desolation round here is that when you finally get to Levisham station, you know

Opposite: *BR No. 80135 forging towards the bend at Darnholm on its way to Pickering.*

Above: *A leisurely wait for the train at Pickering station.*

Above: *The picturesque station house at Levisham.*

Opposite: *Pickering bound, BR class No. 80135 threading its way through Newtondale Gorge.*

that Levisham is still out of sight – it's a large village one and a half miles away and at least 300 feet higher over the rim of the valley. Down here on the line you feel that there's another world somewhere out of sight on both sides, and that the only real world is what you can see from the track.

Up in Levisham it's a different story. I stayed there once, at the Horseshoe pub, near Christmas time for the very different purpose of taking part in a cabaret at Castle Howard. Snowy it was, so much so that the taxi driver who took us across to the Castle preferred to stay there the whole evening and then take us back rather than head for home and get lost in the grounds. When we got back, late, the Horseshoe residents were still up drinking and I remember getting in conversation with a small man who confessed to me (under very little pressure) that he was travelling incognito; he was the head of Islington's controversial housing department and was having a weekend off from red-hot socialism. What I don't remember was any feeling of the presence of the railway. Up there, on the adjoining plateau, where everything tends to face away from the valley, you were on a different level, the real, visible world. Down there in the valley, if there was a line, it was about as visible as the London Underground.

That is at once the pleasure and the limitation of the line, that it is not on top of the moors, but in a secret world of its own, which passes through the moors at a lower level – monarch of all it surveys. The occasional ruined house is spotted on the edge, but that's all until you get to the top and see the three huge golf balls of Fylingdales in the distance, and even they are due to be phased out, I am told, as their useful days of spotting the enemy are almost over. Everyone is rather fond of them by now. If plans were made to remove them, be sure a preservation movement would spring up from somewhere.

The extraordinary thing, once you're over the summit of 550 feet and gliding down towards Goathland, is that although you feel you've been fighting for height for the last ten miles rising above the tree level, getting nearer and nearer what may surely be a lunar waste on top, when you finally do get there you find you are back in quite gentle farmland again. How can you go *up* through such wild country to find farms on top? No matter – we are coming to a stop in Goathland now and I am getting off, as I want to trace the track of the old 1 in 10 incline, and maybe sit and enjoy the deserted station for a moment. No such luck. Normally, these stations on steam lines clear magically as soon as the train has gone, leaving, at most, one enthusiast photographing a milk churn. Here, long after the train has steamed away down the slope to Grosmont, the trippers in their anoraks and rainproof gear – it's midsummer and the forecast is good, but you never know on the moors – are still milling around the station, like racing pigeons which have been released but won't go away. In the small station café the tea-urn is steaming, the trippers are steaming inside their macs, people are buying guidebooks to tell them where to go next, and I am getting a cup of tea and the most enormous biscuit I have ever seen. North Yorkshire Moors Railway Footplate Biscuit it says on its see-through packet, made by E. Botham and Sons of Whitby. Delicious. When I am manager I shall order more of Mr Botham's biscuits.

The only man on the entire station who seems to have acquired any privacy is the signalman, so I decide to go and disturb it. With the possible exception of drivers, who get chatted up far too often, everyone on a preserved steam line who looks wrapped up in his own business is more often that not longing to stop for a chat. The signalman is no exception. He moves his dog over, sits me down and tells me his life story, which involves a strange transition from farming. He was a farmer for sixteen years but became increasingly ill because, it turned out, he was allergic to almost everything that grew on farms. So he went on the railway (his father had been a railwayman in the old days) when it was just getting started.

'Most people in those days thought the NYMR

6619
88
66XX
ABERCYNON

wouldn't succeed,' he says, 'so they wouldn't commit themselves to working on it. I'm glad I did. I wouldn't swap it for anything now. And lots of people who'd like to get jobs on the railway but can't wish they'd come in earlier like me.'

From the signal box just above the station you can see how the slope below the station does get appreciably steeper, as if the trains slowly tip off the edge of the earth like ships going over the horizon. To accommodate any runaway trains there's an escape route half-way down, a siding which goes into a huge sand bunker. Did he think he would ever need it? He smiles.

'I've used that already. Not for a whole train, but for four coaches which escaped from a siding higher up the line. I looked up and there they were, four coaches coming towards me with nobody on board and only me to stop them going dowm into Grosmont station at one hundred miles per hour.'

It's a good story. He tells it well. I can almost see the runaway train. I'm glad it's not me.

'The first thing I can do is put on the traps before it gets to the bridge, but then I realise that if I do that, there's a chance it may derail and demolish the bridge which would be disastrous, seeing as it takes the main road. So I let them run for a while into the station to see if they would slow down, which they didn't, so I pulled the points and let them run into the sand drag, which is supposed to take anything you can throw at it. I was interested to see if the coaches actually would stop, because I'd never seen the drag tested before.'

Very cool, to have just stood there and wondered. Will they stop or won't they? *And* did they?

'Two coaches stopped all right, two went through the sand and then stopped. It was a spectacular sight, I can tell you.'

This man is cool. When I am manager, I will promote him. He will probably refuse promotion, insisting on staying in his signal box with his dog. I will agree to this, but insist on increasing his ration of Footplate Biscuits.

Before I leave his box, I watch a train come blowing up the slope, drawn by *Dame Vera Lynn*, and a spectacular sight it is, the smoke erupting and hanging in the sky as if it were a volcano on wheels. I also ask him the question I most often ask people: What other lines do you approve of beside this one? (SVR, NYMR and Festiniog are the most common answers.) But all he says is that he wouldn't leave this line for any other in the country, not even to visit. This one has got everything.

I bicycle down to Grosmont, stopping only to mend a puncture, and find hundreds more people milling about the station, the sheds, the bookstall, everywhere. It was much quieter up there on the old railway, mending the puncture, and it is with difficulty that I find a seat on the return train. But miracles do occasionally happen and the driver, who has recognised me from one of those television programmes, offers me an impromptu footplate ride on Number 841.

How can I resist? The only thing better than a footplate ride is an unexpected footplate ride, and the whole journey passed in a blur of noise, smoke, vibration, heat, dirt and a loud booming sound which turned out to be the driver, Mike, trying to talk above every other noise. It was curious, passing through Goathland, to reflect that in the signal box I had felt like the king of a small kingdom controlling anything a train or runaway coach wanted to do, whereas from the cab of a big black engine the signal box looked remote, unimportant. Your view of a railway depends a great deal on where you are looking from. From the manager's office you see – problems? worries? complaints? early retirement?

'What's Les's Leap?' I yelled. He yelled back. I couldn't hear him. But he did tell me later about Palmer's Halt, another little landmark along the line. Palmer was a driver who thought he had enough coal for the return trip. He didn't. Palmer's Halt is where he ran out of steam. There is nothing a driver likes better than another driver's mishap or foolishness.

Back in Pickering, I adjourned to the café to write up my notes, and gradually became aware of another

Opposite: *The Grosmont station-master talking to the driver of No. 6619.*

figure at a nearby table, also scribbling away. He looked up at me.

'Miles!' he said.

It was Andy Elliot, a photographer, who had gone out with me and John Bellwood on the Stirling single-wheeler and who lived locally. John Bellwood had died recently, he said. Later he himself had got quite involved with the line, and I suddenly realised with a cold feeling why he was scribbling away at the next table; he, too, was putting in his application for the manager's job. Oh well, it was only fair the job should go to a local man. Anyway, the only real perk of the job would be a free footplate ride, and I had already got that.

When I returned home, I wrote one letter. It was to Mr Botham of Whitby, asking if he sold any of his excellent North Yorkshire Moors Railway Footplate Biscuits by post. Mr Botham wrote back, enclosing free samples of some of the other biscuits he made. There was the Bluebell Railway Footplate Biscuit, the Severn Valley Railway Footplate Biscuit, the Didcot Railway Centre Footplate Biscuit .... They all had different engines on the front and different loco statistics on the back, but they were all the same biscuit.

Above right: *Pickering station – the start of the line.*

Left: *GWR No. 6619 negotiating the last bend of Newtondale Gorge.*

Right: *Remote Levisham station – a starting point for many hikers.*

7 The Jekyll and Hyde Line

The Torbay and Dartmouth Railway

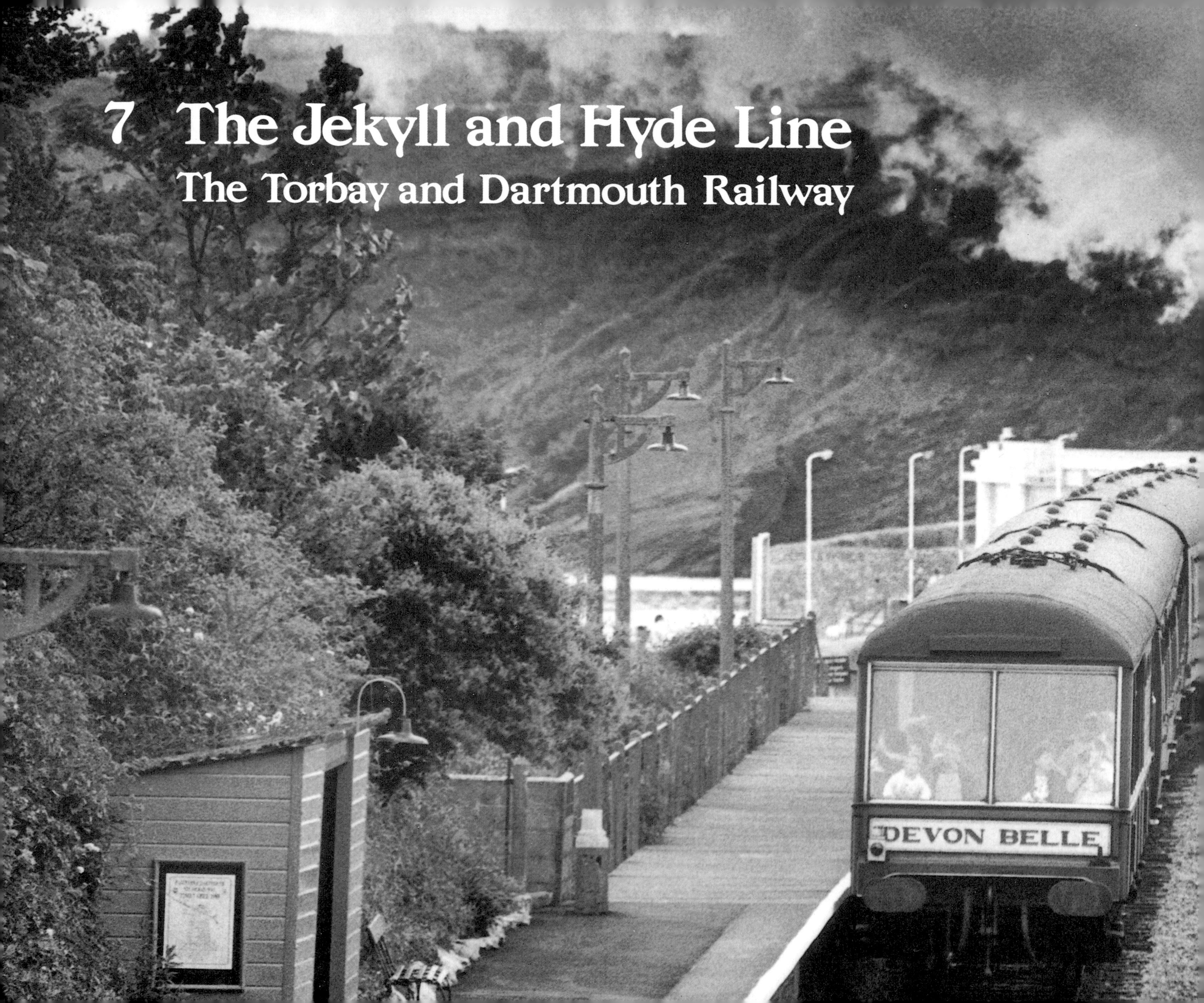

DO NOT CROSS THE LINE
EXCEPT BY MEANS
OF THE FOOTBRIDGE

GREAT WESTERN
DEVON BELLE
SADIQ
23

I ONCE spent a morning fishing on the beach at Goodrington Sands. It was not an experience I would care to repeat. We were paying tribute, for the *Steam Days* series, to the palmy days when the Great Western Railway took millions of holidaymakers down to the Devon Coast and the Cornish Riviera. The Torbay and Dartmouth Railway, running from Paignton to Kingswear, is the only line down there where you can still glimpse steam trains running beside bathing huts, and Goodrington Sands is the station where they get off the train to get into their bathing huts, so it was a logical place to be.

Yet, I couldn't help feeling on that grey, chilly summer morning, as I huddled in my deck chair, that something had vanished since those palmy days. The palms, for a start. And it seemed to me that the families playing cricket were doing it to keep warm, that the other families eating ice-cream were eating ice-cream because that's what you did on holiday, and that what were being doled out as Sun Traps were actually being used by everybody as Wind Shields. People were going about clad only in trunks in weather conditions which, at home, would have them reaching for the central heating switch. Nobody even seemed to mind that Goodrington Sands, which are described in the brochure as 'golden', are in fact a dull reddish colour, as you would expect from that part of Devon with its characteristic stone.

The reason for all this, I suppose, is that if the British are to make holidays in Britain work at all, they have to pretend that something is what it is not, to accept that the label is not always the same as the contents, to believe two things at the same time. And every time I have been along the Torbay and Dartmouth Railway I have had to do the same thing. It is a railway with a split personality, a Jekyll and Hyde of a railway, which

Left: 'Lydham Manor' *(GWR Manor class 4-6-0 No. 7827) follows the River Dart estuary bound for Paignton.*

Previous page: *The Devon Belle observation saloon recedes from Goodrington Sands station.*

Right: 'Lydham Manor' *pulls in at Kingswear station.*

Above: *A view of the Dart Estuary from the carriage window.*

starts off in one country and ends, only seven miles away, in an entirely different place. It's so startling a change as to be dramatic. No, melodramatic. It's so melodramatic as to be either breathtaking or very funny, depending what mood you are in.

The railway starts at Paignton, where the TDR station lies side by side with the BR station, where in turn the line from the rest of the world ends. Paignton is a neat, lower-middle, upper-working sort of a place, with rows of low terraced houses, a feeling of restrained gaiety down the main street and a promenade where people can enjoy themselves without going overboard. In many of the boarding houses at 6 p.m. the soup is served to start off the evening meal, and if you get in at 6.20 you'll have to go straight to the main course. You can still trace here the custom whereby different parts of Britain closed down their factories at different points in the summer, because every time I've been to Paignton I've asked: 'Who's here this week?' and they always know what I mean, saying: 'The Scots all went home yesterday', or 'I think they're getting in from Birmingham on Saturday'. Look at the timetables at the BR station, and you'll find that most of the trains are local but that during the summer you can get a direct train to Newcastle-upon-Tyne, light years away, and on summer Saturdays you can catch a train direct from Paignton to *Scotland*.

Opposite: 'Lydham Manor' *in Kingswear station with Dartmouth on the far side of the River Dart.*

Cross over to the TDR station, and you can get a direct train to Kingswear and Dartmouth, also light years away. For three and a half miles the train chugs along the seafront and up into the hills behind the headland. After stopping at Churston (the only place on the line where you can cross the train coming the other way) you go into a deep cutting, descend into a tunnel, and then – shazam! You're out of Paignton Place and into Happy Valley. Before you is the vista of a deep wide valley, well-lined with trees, with magical rows of boats bobbing at anchor and an old town nestling in the foothills opposite. It's got a bit of the Norwegian fjords and a bit of the Mediterranean and a smattering of Daphne du Maurier's *Frenchman's Creek* and a look of about half a dozen romantic films you've seen. But whatever it reminds you of, it's a conjuring trick the like of which no other railway in Britain can produce.

Even when you know perfectly well what's going to happen, it's still breathtaking, which is the test of the best conjuring tricks. And you know that there is still more to come, because although the train now runs down over a viaduct, down through quiet woods and along the side of the River Dart, where the boats ride at anchor under a season's worth of seagull droppings – there must be a fortune in guano on those covered yachts – you still have the pleasure of getting out at Kingswear and the considerable thrill of taking the ferry over to Dartmouth. Kingswear has a pretty station, which was used for scenes in the film of *The French Lieutenant's Woman*, and a pretty position on one side of the hilly estuary, but not even the keenest Kingswearian could deny that Dartmouth, 200 yards across the water, is the real gem.

Dartmouth has all the quaint things that Paignton hasn't: timbered houses, overhanging eaves, tiny back streets, an old square half-filled with a tidal

NEW QUAY & BOAT HOIST
DARTHAVEN MARINA
WALCON
John Shelbourne
GREAT WESTERN

STATION
REFRESHMENT ROOM
GENTLEMEN
LADIES ROOM
ROOM
LYONS' CAKES
BRUNEL BUFFET
7827

basin, restaurants in *The Good Food Guide*, pubs in *The Good Pub Guide*, lovely little delicatessens in *The Lovely Little Delicatessen Guide*, boats coming and going, green fields at the back of the town, and a feeling of slight mystery round each corner. It has the Britannia Royal Naval College, the Eton of the navy, perched over one side of the town like a presidential palace. It has history, long pages of it, dating back to the time when Devon seamen were loved, loathed and feared the world over, or to the time when Dartmouth was passingly considered for developing as a North Atlantic port, and although Southampton was chosen instead (narrow escape, there) Dartmouth did for a while have sailings every month to the West Indies and Bombay. It knows it's got all this, and is a bit smug about it, and a bit posh and twee, but even though the coach parties are beginning to discover it, Dartmouth's still a gem, for the moment.

When you're in Dartmouth, you can hardly visualise a place like Paignton. Do those little bijou toy streets, like a 1930s building set, really exist? Can a place seem to be so lacking in history? Once back in Paignton, you're through the other side of the looking-glass, and find it hard to believe in Dartmouth. Can a place be so *full* of history? Can a place which looks so much like Heritage-on-Sea have grown naturally? And are they really linked by only seven miles of railway track?

The truth is that one couldn't have the impact it does without the other. If you dropped down into the mouth of the river Dart from an incidental sweet little valley next door, you would hardly notice it, and if you arrived in Paignton by road from Torquay, which I don't recommend, you could hardly keep awake. But just as Dr Jekyll would be just another medic without Mr Hyde, and Lord Greystoke is a bit more interesting because of Tarzan, so Paignton and Dartmouth are inseparable unidentical twins. Dartmouth becomes twice as picturesque, even spectacular, because you're arriving from Plain Jane Paignton, yes, but you appreciate the warmth, homeliness and down-to-earthiness of Paignton that much more coming from a place like Dartmouth where you always have a nagging feeling of keeping your voice down as if in church.

None of which has much to do with *why* the railway was originally built. The stretch from Paignton to Kingswear was opened in 1864, the last link in a rail route taking you all the way back to Paddington which had unfolded fitfully during the mid-nineteenth century. (It had taken eleven years just to complete the link from Newton Abbot to Paignton.) The railway network in Devon and Cornwall spread rather like the high tide coming up a sand-rippled beach, filling in a gap here, linking two places there, running down a vacant valley there, but beyond Kingswear it couldn't go. Even if permission was forthcoming to build a bridge across the Dart to Dartmouth – and it wasn't – the land beyond was not, definitely not, railway country. It was all ups and downs, long estuaries, cliffs and nowhere worth going to.

Opposite: 'Lydham Manor' *in Kingswear station which is decked out with flags to celebrate the anniversary of the arrival of the Torbay and Dartmouth Railway into Kingswear 125 years before.*

Below: 'Lydham Manor' *negotiating a curve on its way through the Devon countryside.*

Opposite: *crossing the Churston Viaduct,* 'Lydham Manor' *heads for Kingswear.*

So Kingswear became the end of the line, and although people still living there will tell you how wonderful it was to get into a train at Kingswear and know you didn't have to get out until you were in London W2, that end of the line was always a bit different. It always remained a single line, after Paignton, for instance, so that the mighty main line expresses which ventured down there were subject to all the provincial bother of passing places and turntables. And when the tide of railways began to turn thirty or forty years ago, and they ebbed back down the beach, closing a line here, cutting off a connection there, drying up a destination yonder, it was the bit from Paignton to Kingswear that was given the thumbs down, condemned in 1972 to becoming a ghost railway.

By a happy chance, the company which was running the nearby Dart Valley Railway from Buckfastleigh to Totnes felt it was in a position to take over from BR. BR agreed. And so the Paignton to Kingswear line became the first and only line to be taken straight from BR in running order for steam preservation, without the regulation intervening period of about five years for miracle-working by volunteers. Considerable work was needed to rearrange and rebuild the station at Paignton, which suddenly had to serve two railways, not one, and British Rail had pulled down quite a lot of the facilities at Churston which are only being replaced now. Basically however, it was a going railway at birth.

Now, I don't know if the Dart Valley Railway people had trouble with split personality before 1972, but they couldn't help it afterwards. Not only had they taken over a line with wildly different extremities – split ends trouble, perhaps – but they had acquired one as different as possible from the one they already had, the one between Totnes and Buckfastleigh being a tiny branch line, calling at no holiday resorts and never having seen a direct train to Paddington in its life. The Torbay line has always made a much healthier profit and carried more passengers than the Dart Valley line, so much so that it tends to subsidise the Dart Valley line. And there even came to be a difference in the character of the volunteers who worked on each line; the Dart Valley volunteers tending to be more traditionalist, that is to say, more pedantic, more worried about authenticity and doing things as they used to be done, whereas on the Torbay line they seemed more concerned with running a railway. When they acquired the Torbay line, they couldn't even decide what to call it – first it was the Torbay Steam Railway, and then the Torbay and Dartmouth Railway which is its official title today, so why on earth on their very own current timetable do they call themselves the Paignton and Dartmouth Steam Railway?

Actually, they have a split personality built into their own constitution. The little Dart Valley line, closed in 1962 and reopened in 1969, after the customary half dozen years of volunteer miracles, was not only masterminded by a consortium of local businessmen but was conceived, right from the start, as a business proposition which had to pay its way and be properly staffed. This is not true of any other steam preserved line – all the others started with a bias towards unpaid volunteers and enthusiasts. The Dart Valley Railway plc, as it is now, always insisted on being a professional set-up. Only – and it's a big only – only, like all other lines, it couldn't survive without keen volunteers. To have a business venture which couldn't operate without volunteer labour is, to put it mildly, double thinking.

Barry Colgar, the present manager, is I think the first full-time manager who has come up through the ranks of the volunteers, so he has the best possible chance of bridging the gap, though when I was trying to track him down I found he has a heaven-sent alibi in trying to run two railways – when they say, I'm sorry, Mr Colgar's on the other line, they mean *railway* line. Yet I didn't find it difficult to detect the presence of the nine-to-five element on both railways. At Paignton, when I turned up on my bike (always bring your bike in the car, park your car round the corner,

GREAT WESTERN

get the bike out and make it seem you've pedalled for 200 miles, never fails to impress, except at Paignton) and made to enter the car-park by the station, I was halted by a lady who stepped forward stridently and said: 'And where do you think you're going to put that bicycle?' Which was a little different from the more normal: 'Bike, mate? Just stick it over there.'

'I am not putting it anywhere. I'm taking it on the train with me.'

'You know you'll have to pay extra, don't you?'

A quid for seven miles, as it turned out. And on the train, where I had become used to chatty guards always willing to unburden themselves to the public, I found that the TDR guard retreats behind a door marked defiantly PRIVATE. But I didn't feel put on until I approached the ticket office at Buckfastleigh on the other line and asked for a return, with bike, to Totnes. She sold me a return to Totnes, and charged extra for the bike. Fair enough. Except that when the train got to Totnes, I couldn't get out of the station with the bike, as there is no exit from the platform for passengers. I had been charged full fare to a station where a bicycle was useless. I think she might have mentioned that at the time.

Well, yes, I suppose I should have known myself, but for the last three years the Dart Valley Railway *had* been steaming into Totnes main line station, had finally restored full diplomatic relations with the old kingdom. It must have been a wonderful moment, psychologically, when Buckfastleigh was reunited with mother, and British Rail finally offered terms which the Dart Valley Railway could accept for getting back into Totnes station, instead of stopping just outside. It even provided the first ever link between the two railways owned by the DVR. You could start out at Buckfastleigh, get off at Totnes, then walk to the quay and get on a river boat (tide permitting) and go all the way down to Dartmouth, where you could ferry over and get on the other train to Paignton.

Right: *Paignton bound,* 'Lydham Manor' *passes the waterside caravan park with the cliffs of Torbay behind.*

Wonderful, except for the small matter of your car still being in Buckfastleigh.

But the passenger traffic generated by the Totnes connection did not maintain its early spurt. British Rail made the terms harsher for getting in. And after three years, in 1989, the DVR decided not to go on steaming into Totnes. It must have been as a big a psychological blow as it had been a boost before. If I'd been in charge, I would have gone to British Rail roaring: 'Look, we've got enough personality confusion and split identities at the DVR already – don't do this to us! Don't deprive us of our link with mother!' At which point men in white coats would have taken me away, so perhaps it's as well that they just settled for stopping short of Totnes again, at a tiny wayside halt where people could get on to the platform, watch the engine run round and then get back in again. But Totnes, hovering just out of reach across the fields, has never looked so inviting.

There was a lone volunteer on the paltform when I arrived, painting a fence.

'How did you get there?' I asked him. 'Is there a footpath to here?'

'No.'

'Then what is there?'

'Nothing. It's all private property round here.'

'Then how?'

'I trespassed.'

But there are compensations. At Buckfastleigh, next to the station car-park, there is a butterfly farm. I have never been to a butterfly farm. I had never even thought about it. But, in I went for a stiff £2, into an enormous greenhouse full of exotic plants, moist, hot tropical air and the most amazing butterflies. I had imagined vaguely that they would be in captivity or behind wire netting, but no – they mingle with the visitors freely. Indeed, they fly round at an average height of five or six feet, at eye level, so that it is like

Left: *Climbing away from the River Dart 45XX class 2-6-2T No. 4555 runs across the Maypool Viaduct.*

Right: *Kingswear and Dartmouth station with a view of Dartmouth across the river.*

C1
GREAT WESTERN
4555

being surrounded by miniature First World War flying machines, crazily painted and on daredevil missions. There is something extremely restful about being surrounded by these trusting creatures – is it my imagination or do they fly in straighter lines, zigzag less often, than our garden butterflies? – and although you are only meant to come in, have a good look and go away again, I think the best way of using the butterfly farm would be as a cheap summer holiday place. If you went in early in the day with a pile of magazines, found a quiet corner and lazed away the time till tea, the £2 would start to seem extremely reasonable for a trip to the tropics.

And even if Totnes is dead, there are other stations. Well, there is Staverton, where I did get off with my bike, a genuinely charming station where I spent a while chatting to this week's volunteers. There is something incredibly relaxing about abandoning a train and watching it disappear fussily into the distance, as if it is somehow taking all your cares with it, then wallowing in the bird-filled silence it leaves behind. Looking after the station is at once a job and a holiday; the arrangement was that whoever came would get a week free, as long as they did the station jobs. Chap last week was a headmaster from Coventry, it was just his bad luck that the lavatory blocked up while he was here, because then it was down to him to clear it. Week before, it was a family from South Wales, that was their summer holiday.

The railway is the only method of following the Dart River down this way, says the brochure. Not quite. I used to know the stretch quite well, as my brother Stewart had a farm overlooking the railway near Buckfastleigh, where he grew crops and cattle on purpose and tomatoes by accident. That was weird. The first summer he was there, a long line of tomato plants appeared growing right across the main lawn in front of the house. Nobody had planted them. Where had they come from? It turned out that there was a cracked sewage pipe going across the lawn. Tomato pips go unscathed through the human body, but if they get the chance to escape from a sewage pipe and germinate, they'll take it.

One day, looking down into the valley, where normally only the train puffed up and down, I saw an outrageous procession passing down the river itself, looking from the distance like an army of clowns from some Fellini film. I ran to investigate. It was the annual raft race, run for charity, entered into lightly but at this stage of things looking desperately hard work. Gangs of rugby forwards dressed as women, men in dishevelled city suits, teams dressed as mountaineers or wine waiters, dragged, pushed, floated and swore at their home-made rafts down a river far rockier than they could have imagined. Bits fell off and were deposited at our feet. Sailors rushed up to us, grabbed those bits, lashed them on to their boat and were off again. Girls who had started out as passengers were suddenly working their passage. This strange apparition, a totally crowded river in a totally deserted landscape, like a bad dream from a Bergman film, is possibly the most unreal thing I have ever seen.

Opposite: *Bunker – first, Great Western No. 4555 pulls past the holidaymakers on Goodrington Sands.*

Below: *Winding through the Lower Dart valley,* 'Lydham Manor' *makes for Kingswear.*

25
PRIVATE FORESHORE
DHNA

But I would agree that, apart from the local raft race, the railway is the best way of seeing the River Dart. I even, on one train, spotted a guard taking a photograph of it. That was impossible. Volunteers are too dignified to take photos. Guards are too grand to take photos. 'Not me, sir' he said cheerfully. 'I like to keep records of the passing seasons here.'

Ah, he wasn't photographing the railway, so that didn't count. But the two families with whom I travelled in the observation coach were much more typical of railway enthusiasts, or at least the fathers were; they had photographic memories. Why this should be, I don't know, but railway enthusiasts have a tremendous visual memory for numbers, shapes, sights, films, photos, videos. I know, because although I always go totally unrecognised elsewhere, on steam lines there are always a few who whip round at the sight of me and say: 'Miles Kington, I've got the programme you did on the Duchess of Hamilton, it was very nice, except I think you made a mistake about...', which is what they really wanted to say.

Both of these families recognised me. They basked in a common link. Made friends with each other and chatted. I asked one father what brought him to the Dart Valley.

'I always like to get on to a steam line on a holiday Saturday,' he said. 'If I don't, I'll get dragged off shopping by her ladyship and that's ten times worse than steam trains.'

His wife laughed, but the other wife looked daggers.

'I think that's the most incredibly sexist thing to say,' she snapped.

The two families were instantly strangers again. And any tendency I might have had to smugness at being recognised was cured the next day when I was paying by cheque at a nearby farm shop for some meat and cider.

'Miles Kington, eh?' said the woman, studying the signature.

'Yes, actually.'

'You must be Stewart's brother, then.'

It was on the Torbay and Dartmouth Railway that I came across something I didn't think existed; a funny railway story written down. Railway stories are funny enough in the pub, and the later it is the funnier. Like opera stories, they almost all concern accidents, disasters or bad mistakes committed by someone known to all present. Told well, they're a hoot. Written down, they're about as amusing as a slow description of a custard pie being thrown. For instance, in *125 Glorious Years,* the booklet published in 1989 to celebrate the birth of the Paignton to Kingswear Line in 1864, John Mann reminisces about incidents from the railway's past and contributes a perfect example of how not to raise a smile.

> To wash coaches we used to throw buckets of water over them, to try to get them clean. In the first instance we didn't have full length hoses. I remember one memorable occasion when dear old Ernie was walking one side smoking his cigar, Yours Truly was the other side with a bucket of soapy water – this certainly put his cigar out!

Hmm. Yet on the next page he describes an episode which is almost worth filming. One day, after the last run, he and his driver, Jesse, were raking out the fire, clearing away the ash, etc., from the engine. To save time they were also refilling the water tank with the hose on full pressure from the mains, but by the time they had cleaned out the fire and moved off ('a lot of people don't realise that an engine will run for some time after the fire is chucked out,' he adds) they'd forgotten all about the water.

'As the engine toddled down the track, Yours Truly noticed something which appeared to be a piece of electric cable, orange in colour, and I thought: "I wonder who put that there, don't remember that there before!" In point of fact, it was our hosepipe stretching thinner and thinner. The next thing we knew, there was a low rumbling under the ground and something passed the engine at great speed: it was actually the tap to which the hose was attached

Opposite: *The start of the return journey to Paignton along the River Dart estuary.*

together with the standpipe and the water main! It missed the engine cab by inches.'

They immediately reversed up the line to see how bad the trouble was. 'It was a hot day and the engine cab roof was slid back, and of course by that time Vesuvius itself had erupted in water right up through the ground and it was beginning to rain like Niagara all over the trees. We reversed into this. The comical thing was that Jesse, like many Great Western men, always wore cycle clips, and his overall, bibs and brace immediately filled with water and he looked rather like Coco the Clown.' The story, which Hoffnung would have relished, ends with the park next door turning into a lake and the schools sports being abandoned.

(He also has a very appealing story of the crossing keeper near Kingswear who liked to go fishing in between opening the gate for trains. However, one day he miscalculated the tides and as the train came to the closed crossing, hooting furiously, the driver could see a frantic keeper vainly attempting to row back to land against the current.)

Right: *Great Western No. 4555 hugging the River Dart estuary on its journey between Britannia Halt level crossing and Kingswear.*

Below: *Having taken water,* 'Lydham Manor' *steams out of Paignton station.*

Off the Rails
7827
PASSENGERS MUST
NOT TRESPASS
ON TRACK

I have mentioned before the importance to small steam railways of the filming done on their lines – I asked several of them for quotes, and the charges generally came to about £1,000 a day, everything thrown in – but it was only on the TDR that I actually saw any going on. The station at Kingswear had been renamed Looe for the filming of an episode in the *Poirot* television series, and the station approach was suddenly full of men with pencil moustaches and chauffeur's hats, looking rather rat-like, and women with posh travelling clothes and lovely brown luggage. If there is one thing I have learnt in life, it is that watching filming is the most boring activity known to man, so I passed over to Dartmouth immediately on the ferry. Not the pedestrian ferry, the car ferry, as bikes are forbidden on the pedestrian one, though I was interested to note that I got across much quicker on the car ferry, which doesn't take so long to load. A handy tip for pushed pedestrians.

By leaving my car at Paignton and arriving at Dartmouth on bike, I had accidentally done a Jekyll and Hyde the wrong way round: arrived at Paignton looking smart, arrived at smart Dartmouth humping two red bike bags. And it was one of the smart nights of the year, too, being the passing-out ball at Britannia Royal Naval College, with the town full of young men with Prince Andrew haircuts, all towing adoring parents or glistening girlfriends or both. The pubs were all full, the restaurants crowded, and I was lucky to get the last room at the Royal Castle Hotel, not a grand room at the front but a tiny room at the back, which is infinitely preferable if your grand room at the front is likely to overlook young men with Prince Andrew haircuts making a lot of noise until the early hours.

I ate next door at Taylor's restaurant, specialising in fish, and not just fish but such fish as John Dory, bass, brill and porbeagle shark, done with fennel, mint, lemon etc. ('We're beginning to get good trade now, sir, but it took a while as the establishment previously had a very bad name, being part of the local drug scene....') and reflected yet again on the schizophrenic difference between Paignton and Dartmouth. Paignton for fish and chips, Dartmouth for porbeagle shark. I reflected on the strange mentality of the railway, half-demoralised, half-bright and bouncy, half-keen-as-mustard volunteers, half-jobsworths. I reflected on the ticket collector who, when I told him I was after facts, said: 'Do you mean the official facts, or the real facts?' I reflected on how manager Barry Colgar had told me that the Dart Valley Railway had been the first line to introduce Dining Specials but that they had discontinued them, and told myself that only the Dart Valley Railway could have pioneered them at a time when they were a novelty and then given them up at a time when they proved to be a money-earner second only to Santa Specials.

After which, fed up with reflecting, I tucked into my porbeagle shark. Excellent. The next morning I jumped on my bike and rode up the back of Dartmouth, which nearly killed me, and came out on a back lane overlooking miles of empty countryside, rolling mysteriously away towards Salcombe or Kingsbridge, places I knew nothing of, except that between me and them there were no railways and never had been. I put my head down and set off.

Opposite: *Letting off steam: the* 'Lydham Manor' *at Paignton station.*

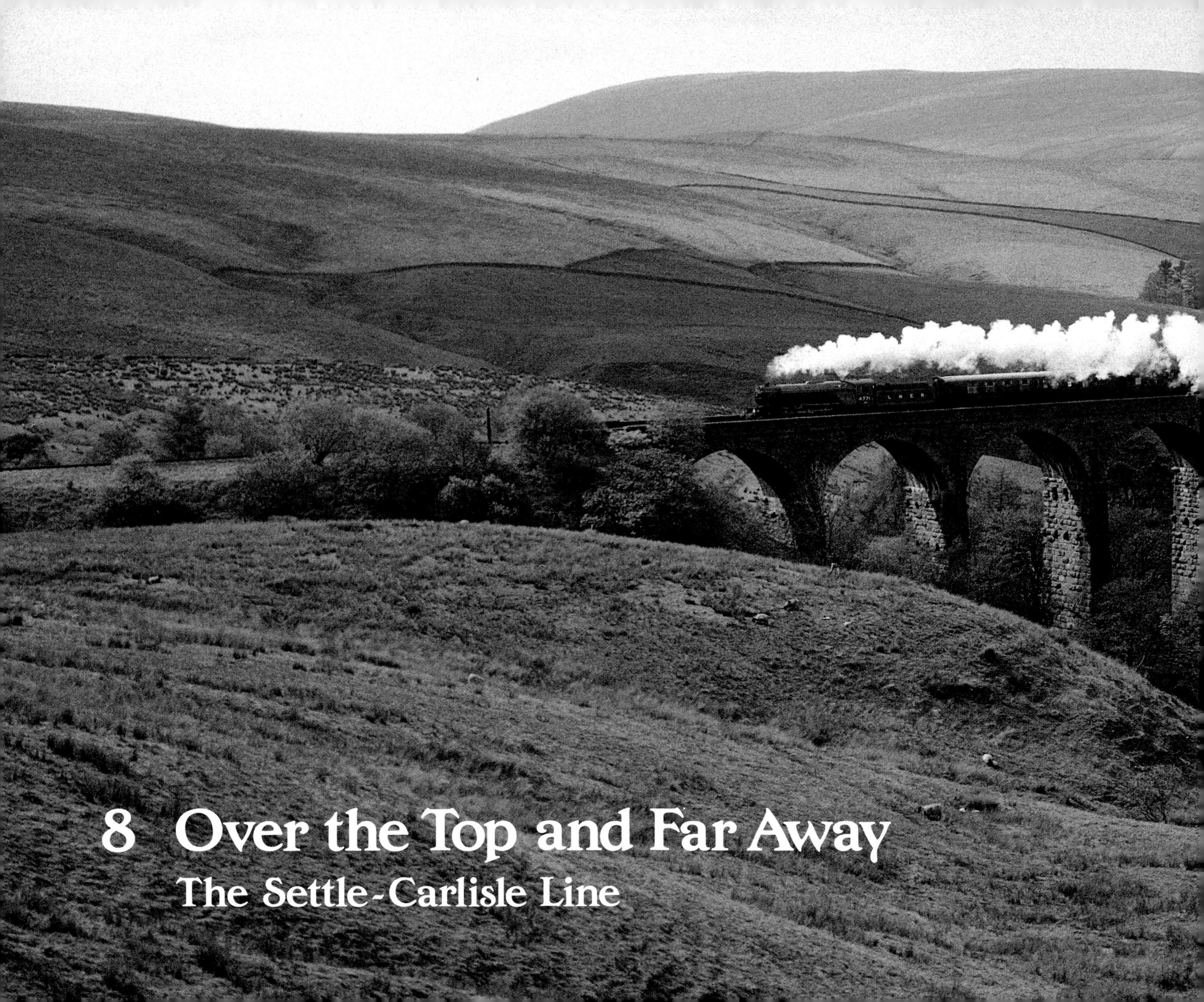

8 Over the Top and Far Away

The Settle-Carlisle Line

L M S

Above: *Merchant Navy 4-6-2 No. 35028* 'Clan Line' – *locos of this type were used on the crack expresses of BR's Southern Region.*

Previous page: *LNER* 'Green Arrow' *(2-6-2 class V2 No. 4771) heading south across Dent Head Viaduct.*

Left: *LMS Stanier class 5 No. 5407 climbing south along the side of Mallerstang Valley, passing Sycamore Tree Farm.*

THE BIGGEST mistake you can make with the Settle-Carlisle line is talking about it as if it were a railway. It isn't a railway. It's a symbol. It's the altar-piece of a religion. It's a vast cathedral of railway worship. When steam specials go over the Settle-Carlisle Line today, they are not carrying passengers but pilgrims, pilgrims who are coming to pay tribute to a miracle, the miracle being that the line is open. And if it were just a railway line it would not still be open.

If it were just a railway line, it would never have been built. A railway line is a line that goes from one place to another place for a purpose, and with the best will in the world it is hard to see what purpose is served by having a railway line between Settle and Carlisle, especially one that almost deliberately avoids human habitation *en route*. The amount of people in Settle who want to go to Carlisle regularly, or vice versa, can be counted on the fingers of one mitten. And yet there is something about the Settle-Carlisle Line which turns men's heads to jelly and make them

express themselves in terms of awe. In their book on the line written in 1948, Houghton and Foster wrote:

> Just as we of this generation wonder how those people of ancient Egypt built the Pyramids so will a later generation of dwellers in this island wonder how the Settle-Carlisle Railway was built. Just as we praise the Romans who built The Wall and The Roads so will those who follow after us praise the men who flung this Way of Steam Engine across the Pennine Hills.

Even British Rail, not famous for their prose, have this to say in their latest leaflet:

> The seventy miles from Settle to Carlisle may be not only the most spectacular railway journey in Britain but among the most memorable journeys in the world.

Can this be the very same BR who have been trying to close the line for donkey's years? Can this really compare with the best the Egyptians and Romans had to build? Can seventy miles of upland railway really compare with trains going 16,000 feet in the Andes, through the Canadian Rockies for day after day, or across the interminable plains of Australia? Has everyone gone mad? Are people bewitched by the Settle-Carlisle Line, or what?

I think very possibly they are. And I think this enchantment has been present right from the birth of the line, brought to it by a good fairy in the very unlikely shape of the House of Commons. It's duly noted in histories of the line that the Midland Railway was the mother and father of the Settle-Carlisle, and so it was, but what is less emphasised is that the Midland Railway wanted an abortion. Their great ambition was to have a through route to Scotland. Their access to the pre-existing East and West Coast routes was made so difficult by the owners of those lines that the Midland Railway struck its chest and said, Right! We will build our own line, right up the middle! We will get an Act of Parliament! We will drive a wonderful line from Settle to Carlisle to give us a London-Glasgow route!

And they got their Act of Parliament, but they may have been calling the bluff of the owners of the West Coast route because by the time the Act was on the books, the Midland had come to an arrangement with them which made the Settle-Carlisle line quite unnecessary. So they applied to Parliament for permission to abandon the unstarted line, and the baby would never have been born except that Parliament – which perhaps did not like being mucked about with, or wished to discourage further stop-go railway schemes – refused them permission and insisted they must build the line.

If the Midland Railway made a reluctant parent, it has to be admitted it was a good parent. This birth was hard and the labour lasted six and a half years, instead of the projected four, but the infant railway was sturdy and in good health. Nevertheless, there are other mountainous and wild stretches of railway in Britain, whether north from Inverness, or on the West Highland line, across Wales, or up Shap even. Why is it the Settle-Carlisle Line which, alone among all these

Opposite: 'Cumbrian Mountain Express' *climbing hard as it approaches Sherrif's Brow.*

Below: *Dent Head station caught in the winter evening light.*

lines, has achieved sanctity and become this cathedral on the hills?

Well, for the very simple reason that you don't expect to find a cathedral in the hills and you don't expect to find a line like this in the mountains. Mountain lines almost always are single lines, capable of following tight curves and hugging contours. They tend to meld in with the landscape, to bend and fold with it, to do what they're told, even to go up and down with it. There's a certain poetry, a lyrical quality in the way a branch line sinks into nature.

The Settle-Carlisle Line is quite the opposite. It was an express line, double line, which had to take fast trains and therefore had to be fairly straight, heavily built and pretty flat. The line doesn't do what it's told – it tells the landscape what it wants to do and then does it. There are many places where it could have taken the easy way out and, say, followed the outline of a hill, but instead it has gone striding across on a viaduct, arrogantly, masterfully. Occasionally I have been driving across the Pennines on back roads, quite forgetting that I was going to cross the railway, and it is always an unnerving moment when you encounter this huge line marching across your route. I imagine that Chinese ramblers feel much the same when they come across the Great Wall of China by accident. There is nothing pretty or seductive about the line, nothing loveable, even. It's gaunt, craggy and weather-beaten, like one of those old Western film stars who preferred the company of horses and wild places to women, and shooting their way out of trouble, not talking.

Among British railway lines it's a freak, in the same way that we call a flood a freak when it is the result of several different factors such as high winds, high tides, quick rainfall and bad weather forecasting. The

Opposite: 'Cumbrian Mountain Express' *slogs north through the Pennine mist near Helwith Bridge.*

Below: *The desolate Grisedale Crossing in the heart of the Pennines.*

Above: *No. 35028 waiting for the all clear from the guard at Appleby station.*

Settle-Carlisle Line resulted from a freak combination of corporate pride, Parliamentary stubbornness, Victorian railmania, terrible terrain and the lack of routes to Scotland. Most freak floods abate after a couple of days, but the Settle-Carlisle Line has been going for 120 years now, the last thirty of which it has spent under the threat of closure. Any other line might have been closed by now. The book by Mitchell and Joy on the line in 1966 doubts whether the centenary of the line in 1976 would be celebrated, admits that the line must lose millions of pounds and can see no use for it once Shap is electrified – and yet the line is still open.

This threat of closure, combined with an ability to escape the death sentance, is the other thing that makes the line special. The first time I went on the Settle-Carlisle Line was in the mid-1980s, for a run behind the *Duchess of Hamilton*, on a bleak, grey, scudding day, like most days up there. The train turned right at Carlisle to get to Newcastle and then back to Leeds, but I had to leave the train at Carlisle and return on the next InterCity 125 to London. As I came back over Shap and down the other side, the sun came out for the first time that day and made wonderful mad patterns on the hillsides, which themselves suddenly took on a real grandeur like nothing I'd seen all day. The Settle Line was grim by comparison. And the subversive thought came to my mind: *what if the Settle Line was the agreed main line and Shap was under threat of closure?* What sort of an outcry would there be? Would everyone say how wonderful and unique Shap was, and not talk about the Settle Line at all? On that day, certainly, I felt my pulse race on Shap, and not on the Settle Line, but to say so is almost blasphemous. Is the Settle-Carlisle Line made more glorious by the axe hanging over it, and is it out of all proportion?

I am certainly convinced that there is a peculiar force at work here, which I might call for convenience the Settle-Carlisle Syndrome. It works like this. Somebody wants to make a programme about railways for television. They suggest it about the Settle Line, because it's under threat, or because it's got great viaducts, or because they simply love it. They get in touch with experts on the line, with the Friends of the Settle to Carlisle Railway, with old railwaymen. They don't make a programme about Shap, because Shap will always be there, whereas the Settle Line may not. They don't get in touch with expert historians on the line who hate it, because there aren't any. They don't get in touch with the enemies of the Settle to Carlisle Railway because although there may be some, they don't bother to band together. The nearest they might get is asking someone from British Rail to say that Ribblehead Viaduct is far too expensive to maintain.

So what you end up with is dozens of programmes, radio, film and television, on the Settle Line and none on comparable lines. All the programmes are totally besotted with the line, because people who are not besotted with the line don't make programmes about it, and very few doubts are expressed in them. As a back-up, dozens of books, historians and

Opposite: 'Green Arrow' *storming towards Shotlock Tunnel.*

№ 4771

photographic albums are published on the Settle line and, presumably, bought by the friends and lovers of the line. It's a self-perpetuating, bandwagon, self-obsessed process. It's not confined to the Settle Line – I've seen it happen in Bordeaux wines, opera, Liverpool comedians, J.R.R. Tolkien and the Rolling Stones, among others – but that's where it is seen in its most concentrated form, in railway terms.

This then leads to a slight one-party state situation, in which any criticism is seen as treachery. If I ever mutter under my breath that the Settle line is not the best and finest in Britain, it is taken as tantamount for a plea to have it closed down. I think it would be fearful if it were closed down, but I'm quite happy to let years go by without my clapping eyes on it.

You also end up with the language of the one-party state, in which terms used to describe the line tend to err on the poetic side. Next time you open a book on the Settle-Carlisle line, you might benefit from having this glossary at your elbow to help translate.

Breathtaking = Bleak
Bleak = Desolate
Desolate = Godawful
Magnificent scenery = Godawful conditions for building a railway in
Magnificent and unspoilt scenery = Godawful conditions, far from any road
Exposed = Often closed by snow
Engineering feats = Building bridges and viaducts which are a headache to maintain
Unparalleled engineering feat = Not making the same mistake again
Over the Watershed = Through terrible bogs
Storming up the slope = Having great trouble getting to the top
Remote = Place where nobody wants to live
Remote countryside = Place with no local population to serve by train
Opening up the remote countryside by rail = Sending express trains rushing through areas where nobody lives, without stopping

Above: *Ais Gill Viaduct in that all too common winter Pennine fog.*

There is one bit on the line which is generally agreed even by the high priests to be genuinely grim, and that is in and around the Blea Moor Tunnel, which was intensely disliked by the people who built it and is liked by almost nobody today. The fireman certainly wouldn't like it, because he would be bent over his shovel in choking conditions, knowing that he had another eight or so miles to the end of the Long Drag. The first twenty miles out of Settle were a non-stop gradual climb, which meant twenty miles of non-stop firing. It's hardly surprising that a lot of drivers and firemen welcomed the end of steam, though this too is not often mentioned in the one-party state.

(I met a fireman once who did the London to Glasgow run and had been beseeched at Carlisle by a German passenger to let him come on the footplate for a while. Well, he said, it was late at night and no inspectors around, so he let him hop on as far as Lancaster. The man got off shaking with fear. 'That was the most frightening thing I have ever done in my life, and I speak as someone who was a U-Boat captain

Opposite: 'Cumbrian Mountain Express' *leaves Ais Gill bridge behind after a long, laboured climb towards Ais Gill summit.*

Opposite: 'Green Arrow' *forging south through Wild Boar Fell and on to Ais Gill summit.*

during the war,' said the German, before vanishing. So now you know that driving a steam train is not as romantic as piloting a submarine in wartime, and that there are easier ways to earn a living.)

The Long Drag is highly welcomed by steam enthusiasts, though, because there is something much more spectacular about a train struggling to the top than one coasting down the far side, and the Settle-Carlisle line, like most of the great lines, is high in the middle and low at either end, so whichever end you start, the first half is always the more dramatic. If you're inside the train, there'a a lot more noise and effort. If you're outside, clutching a camera, there's a lot more smoke and steam. Of course, if you're outside in a field photographing the smoke and glory, the disadvantage is that the train will be gone in a minute. But there are speed restrictions on main-line steam trains these days, so there's a good chance you can catch it up in a good car, so you jump in and set off. Unfortunately, lots of other people have the same idea, so a small Grand Prix forms along the B roads, and if you are in the train looking out, you are amazed to see these remote country lanes choc-a-block with some pretty smart cars.... Meanwhile, you are leaning out of the window trying to get a view of the engine and a good shot past all the other heads looking out, and the people with cameras in the field are cursing because everyone in the train is poking his head out, and also they don't want to get in shot the diesel locomotive at the back of the train which is providing the heating which the steam engine can't provide, and they don't want to get in shot all the video cameramen standing in the field next to them nor the sound recordists sticking their mikes in the air....

Below: *Bleak and wintry: Garsdale station resting under the shadow of Baugh Fells.*

Do you know what I think? I think it is wonderful that the Settle-Carlisle Line is still open, and I think it is wonderful that steam trains are still running over it, but I don't think I ever want to go on another steam special again. It's such a dreadful way of seeing steam engines, and seeing the line. Being one-off specials, they are mostly jam-packed, with not enough windows for everyone to stick his head out of. You can hardly see the engine, so at each station everyone gets off, rushes to the front, looks at the engine as if it might have changed colour since the last station, and gets back on again. The countryside is full of people looking back at you and photographing you. If you are a purist you may be worried by the fact that an old steam engine is pulling some not-so-old coaches (with a diesel at the back) down a line it never went down in real life. And worst of all, everyone on the train is a steam enthusiast.

(I have nothing against steam enthusiasts. It's just unnatural to be on a train in which everyone is a steam enthusiast. I once asked Richard Boston, when he was writing a weekly beer column for the *Guardian,* which kind of pub he preferred to go to. 'A Watney's pub,' he said. This amazed me – Watney's was the anti-Christ at the time. 'I know,' he said, 'but you know you won't meet any Real Ale freaks there.' By the same token, I would prefer to go up the Settle Line in a local diesel-hauled train with a few local people on board.)

This is the weird paradox that has overtaken the line

these days. Alone of all the lines in this book it is a mighty, main line with steam running on it. There's nothing preserved or toy-town or playing-at-trains about it. Except for the steam trains themselves, which are all artificially planned, going nowhere, not regularly scheduled and not the kind of train you can just get on when it comes. The preserved lines are all hot-house growths, if you like, which couldn't be run without volunteers and which could be dismissed as little toy railways, yet they *all* have regular scheduled steam timetables and trains that you just get on to as if it were normal to catch a steam train.

That I am not quite alone in this feeling I was glad to learn in an exchange of letters with Nick Lera, a BBC cameraman whose championship of steam has made him many friends – in fact, one of his reminiscences is too good and pointed to waste on a letter. Here it is.

> Back in 1967 I turned out in the sleet and cold to see *Clun Castle* on a special to Carlisle. I drove through the November fog all the way from London to Shap to Witness. My wife rightly thought I was demented. They hadn't even built the M6 then. So I got my camera set up on Shap Fell and started to suffer from hypothermia as the scheduled passing of the *Castle* receded further and further into memory. As dusk approached, a distant whistle could be heard, and at last the train appeared, chuffing magnificently up the gradient. My frozen fingers pressed the camera start switch and I peered through the viewfinder, relieved that my trip had not been in vain after all. After the train had passed I went to take my finger off again and discovered to my horror that it was already off — I had not, it appeared, actually run the camera at all. My hands were so numb with cold I couldn't tell if I had actually pressed the switch or not. So I drove all the way home, thoroughly ashamed of myself and deeply mortified.
>
> It wasn't until some weeks later when I picked up the camera again to reload it for some other special train, that I noticed the footage counter had registered over fifty feet. Then I remembered I had filmed a couple of goods trains to pass the time while I waited for the

Opposite: 'Green Arrow' *crossing the famous Ribblehead Viaduct – the remnants of a medieval forest lie in the foreground.*

4771
L N E R

Castle. I had the film developed, put it away in a can and forgot about it. This film, all one minute twenty seconds of it, is now of course one of the gems in my collection, simply because it shows real steam trains in a real setting doing their real job, and not a train buff in sight. A colleague at work dubbed some sound on it, and the result is a piece of actuality that leaves the audience gasping whenever I show it. The missed *Castle* is of course a mere irrelevance, as are, sad to say, all the steam specials that have been plying the S & C for the last fifteen years.

Well, yes and no. Irrelevant to Nick and to purists who would insist on authenticity, or on steam trains being working steam trains. But you could make a good case out for steam specials having established their own kind of authenticity – 'Oh yes,' people might say in years to come, 'the *City of Wells* used to do specials over the Settle Line, or *Clun Castle* was used for Shap specials, so it would be quite authentic to use them again.' Anyway, I am all in favour of steam specials myself. I just would prefer to be on the little local train going the other way. Or be on a private train pulled by *The Flying Scotsman* with no public aboard.

This, I am glad to say, did happen to me once, when we were engaged in BBC filming in the mid-80s. It was near Christmas, we were making a film about *The Flying Scotsman* and we had been waiting for the engine to get back on its feet all year. Finally, the owners told us it was doing a test run up to Settle and back from Carnforth, and gave us permission (or sold us permission) to come aboard and film. It was a cold, grey day, and the BR inspector was happy to give it the all-clear and tell us to head for home. We had enough light left for a run past at a tiny station on the way home, so we set up the cameras on the bridge, the engine retreated to a distance and then it came flying at us like a long jumper about to take off. But before it could reach the station, something seemed to go wrong; there was a flash, or a crack, among the wheels and the engine started making strange noises. It came quickly to a halt and the volunteers, all the orange-jacketed men, rushed over to inspect it. I can't remember the technical terms, but a vital coupling had broken and the engine was reduced from three pistons to one.

It's said in defence of steam engines that when something goes wrong it can always limp home whereas a diesel will just collapse, and it was true this night. It went along at about 5 mph, jerking painfully and giving off a 'Chuff!' about once every five seconds, but it never stopped. What the BR inspector who had given it the all-clear said, I don't know, but I do remember one of the volunteers saying to the BBC sound recordist that he *had* to record the noise it was now making.

'Why?' said the sound man, who had been recording train noises all day and was fed up. 'What's special about this?'

'Because this is the only chance anyone will ever get to record the sound of *The Flying Scotsman* moving on one cylinder. You've got to! Please... It's historic.'

'Bugger that,' said the sound man, and he wouldn't either, which shows that some people are less impressed by authenticity than others.

More and more steam specials were organised through the 1980s on the Settle-Carlisle as it seemed more likely that the line would be closed. They were very popular, as they would be if everyone thought it was their last chance to travel down that line. If I were in charge of a line, I would issue yearly reports that it was due to be closed down that year and put extra staff in the ticket office. But things got serious when British Rail applied for permission to close the line down (shades of the Midland asking for permission not to start). It wasn't granted as such. Instead, the Transport Minister asked BR to prepare a proposal for the privatisation of the line.

What happened next depends on who you talk to about it. One line of thought says that if only Ribblehead Viaduct, the most monumental but most

Opposite: 'Green Arrow' *blasting through Sheriff's Brow as it climbs north.*

L N E R
4771

Left: 'Green Arrow' *on the monumental Ribblehead Viaduct, now sadly crumbling.*

crumbling one on the line, could be safeguarded, the line would be all right. Others say that it could never have been privatised – there were simply too many problems involved, such as running into Carlisle under electric overhead lines and sorting out safety regulations. A third, and the one I prefer because it contains an element of conspiracy, says that BR used the chance to prove to the government that privatisation wouldn't work. That is, they put the line out to tender as if it were a railway line from Settle to Carlisle, not a historic property and national treasure, and measuring the profit in terms of ordinary traffic.

Not unnaturally, no very good tender was received and the privatisation proposal was withdrawn. Meanwhile, the man whom BR had put in charge of getting ready for closure or at least disposal of the line, Mr Ron Cotton, was letting them down badly. He was making a roaring success of it, promoting traffic and increasing profits. It wasn't just a question of boosting steam outings; they also, for instance, would let it be known on the grapevine that such-and-such a kind of diesel would be pulling such-and-such a train. Now, this would be a diesel that had never been on the line before or had never pulled that kind of train before, and miraculously the train would be jam-packed, where before it had been nearly empty, with diesel fans who had come out of the woodwork just as easily as steam buffs.

On 11 April 1989 Mr Channon announced from the Transport Office that the Settle-Carlisle Line would not be closed by British Rail. An enormous sigh of relief went up from everyone, including the steam operators who had already sold their summer special tickets. Parliament, the good fairy who had insisted on the birth taking place, had completed the trick by forbidding euthanasia in old age, and now we can look forward into the 1990s, wondering if the surge of belief in the line can be maintained, now that the miracle of keeping the line open has been declared official. It is not a line which is easy to love. Fall under the spell of, yes, but not love. Somehow there are too many ghosts of all the men who lost their lives building it, of all the wasted effort trying to fill in bogs which swallowed all the aggregate they were given, of all the construction workers who made the countryside more populous in 1870 than it is now, of all the sleeping passengers who passed from London to Glasgow (six and a half hours in 1900) over the Yorkshire Moors, oblivious even to where they were.

But there are many people who return there again and again, compulsively, and everyone should go on it at least once. Facts about the line, about the viaducts, its bridges, are two a penny and contained in every book, so I have not dealt with them here, but if in the 1990s you should venture that way, here is another vocabulary guide to take with you.

The weather up here is never the same twice = Sometimes it rains, sometimes it doesn't
That mountain over there is Ingleborough = That cloud over there has got Ingleborough inside it somewhere
We are on Ais Gill Viaduct = We are on Ais Gill Viaduct, but you cannot see it, as we are on it
The weather up here in unpredictable = It's raining again
We are at Garsdale = We are at Garsdale Station; there is no place called Garsdale
It is quite unspoilt round here = It is very lonely round here
Lonely = Deserted
Deserted = Godforsaken
Godforsaken = Blea Moor
We are at Dent Station = We are four miles from Dent
The weather is closing in = The wind is blowing the rain harder
It is glorious down here in Eden Vale = It is wonderful not to be on the top any more

3442
L N E R
VICTORIA BRIDGE.
1861.
JOHN FOWLER, ENGINEER.
MESSRS. BRASSEY & CO., CONTRACTORS.

9 How to Succeed After Really Trying

The Severn Valley Railway

Previous page: 'The Great Marquess' *LNER class K4 2-6-0 No. 3442 hauling a Bewdley to Bridgnorth train over Victoria Bridge.*

Opposite: *Early morning and all quiet at Hampton Loade station.*

'THERE ARE grave dangers in seeking to make a commercial organisation out of a body which depends for its success on the co-operation of a large body of subscribing volunteers.' (John Marshall, *The Severn Valley Railway*, 1989, David and Charles)

'Volunteers will do things and get into places I wouldn't even dream of.' (British Rail driver in Fort William)

'Quite honestly, I think I'm the only person working on this railway who's not odd.' (Accountant with famous steam railway)

'Ideally, all preserved steam lines should be run by volunteers and no paid staff. Ideally, *I* should be a volunteer.' (Catering Manager on Severn Valley Line)

'When a volunteer becomes a permanent staff member, he stops working all hours and starts clocking off on the dot.' (Manager of line)

'The young volunteers think they bloody know it all.' (Older volunteer on the Bluebell Railway)

'Don't believe it if anyone tells you he's got enough volunteers. Nobody ever has. We're always desperately short of volunteers.' (Department Head, Severn Valley Line)

'We're never short of volunteers.' (Head of famous steam line)

'All of us volunteers are probably either social or sexual inadequates.' (Man on Festiniog Line)

Below: *A young steam enthusiast enjoying his trip on the Severn Valley Railway.*

I met a great many volunteers while working on this book, and can't remember one I disliked. (The same is not so true of enthusiasts or full-time staff). For some reason, though, it's one or two of the ones I met on the Severn Valley Railway who most stick in my mind, and it's something said by a man in Bewdley station yard which most lingers in my ears.

The reason I always liked talking to volunteers was not just that they were knowledgeable and interesting (not at all the same thing) but also because I became obsessed with finding out what drove them on. Many of them have an unquestioning loyalty to steam, or diesel, or railways, or one particular line, which borders on the religious. Why? Is it perhaps religious in some way? It is partly a sexual substitute, as the Festiniog man suggested (and I couldn't tell from his expression whether he was serious or sending me up)? In his book on the Festiniog line, *The Little Wonder: 150 Years of the Festiniog Railway* (Michael Joseph 1986) (which I reckon to be the best written book on railways I have read for years), John Winton addresses this prickly problem and puts forward the idea that people find in railways a kind of order or structure which would otherwise be missing from their lives, and that other people find even more strongly in the army or prison. Whatever it is, it must be a strong drive that makes men sweat to lay a sleeper, mould a fitting or pull a signal knowing that their effort is taken entirely for granted, both by the traveller and by those who come after.

The man at Bewdley was tall, greying with very bushy hair, and gifted with magnetic eyes set like mysterious cottage windows in the thatch of his hair. I hadn't meant to stop and talk to him at all, but he happened to get up and stretch from his work as I was

2
1
GENTLEMEN

7819

passing. Or maybe I was admiring the engine he was working on, and he was just responding. Maybe it was just his eyes that stopped me. I can't remember now, but I remember the engine number, 7741, and that he had been working on it for eleven years.

'That's mostly weekends, of course, not full-time. There have been some stretches when I haven't worked on it at all – there was a period of eighteen months when I didn't touch it, because that was the time of the big push to Kidderminster, and all hands were needed to get there. The engine still needs, I'd say, about another five years of good work to be in proper running condition.'

I suggested to him that there was a distinct possibility that he might not be around by the time it finally got running again. He might never see the fruit of his works.

'Maybe,' he said, 'but that's not really the point, is it?'

That's the remark which stayed with me. How could a man possibly devote so much time to something which might never happen? Then what *is* the point? Why are you giving up all this time to an inert piece of metal? But before I could ask any of these questions, he was, did I but know it, answering them.

'There are only a few of us working on this little old tank engine, so it's bound to take years. And we have very little money to pay for parts to be made or restored, so we have to do it all ourselves, which means building our own machines, lathes, etc. But before we could do that, we had to build houses for the lathes, and so on. And then add on the time we spent on the last push to Kidderminster, but *that* was worth it too. Building a line is a bit like rebuilding an engine. When the line was reopened it only got as far as Hampton Loade from Bridgnorth, which is four miles or so, then there was a push to get it to Eardington, which seemed a long way at the time, then it was all the way to Bewdley and now this last stretch to Kidderminster.'

So now the line is complete?

'Well, there is always the possibility of going beyond Bridgnorth to Ironbridge. I'm all in favour, myself. I think it's a good thing to have an objective because I've noticed that morale and effort do sag in between targets. You reach Bewdley. You think, Right, we've done it. You slacken right off, so it's good that there's still Kidderminster to get to. But after Kidderminster, what? It's the same with this engine, actually. I can remember the day we finally got the thing back on wheels – we went around with smiles on our faces for weeks afterwards. Then they faded and we got down to the next target.'

Above: *A driver at Bewdley stretching his legs between journeys.*

Above: *Strength is needed to pull those levers at Arley signal box.*

Opposite: 'Hinton Manor', *ex-GWR No. 7819 4-6-0, approaching Highley station.*

Perhaps what he's saying is that it's like going up a mountain when you can't see the top, only the end of the next rise. You get there, and there's another rise to aim at. You get to the top of that, and there's another... and you keep going, even though the thought begins to cross your mind that you'll never see *the* top.

'The great thing about being here in the West Midlands is that with the industrial and railway background there are lots of people around with interest in railways. In the Dorset village I used to live in there were two rail buffs, me and another bloke, and we were both looked on by the other 250 inhabitants as not-quite-grown-up children. Here I am surrounded by kindred spirits, though I have to admit that the wife thinks I'm a bit barmy.'

That's what you have to do, surround yourself with kindred spirits who won't ask you what the point is; they'll *know* what the point is. It's like what Fats Waller said to the old woman who asked him what rhythm was: 'Lady, if you've got to ask, you'll never know.' This man is Fats Waller and I'm the old lady.

Any other question I need to ask will probably be answered by John Marshall's brand new history of the line, all the factual simple stuff like, when was the line closed and when did it reopen? But not so. I read the book a couple of times, and it wasn't mentioned anywhere. It only gradually dawned on me that that was not how it happened at all; the line didn't simply close down and one day reopen a bit later, like a cinema reopening as a bingo hall, but closed down bit by bit and reopened bit by bit. Indeed, there seems to

Stephens
for ALL Fountain Pens
TELEPHONE
BOOKING HALL
7819

have been some time in the late 1960s when the line had been relaunched at one end as a steam line while the other end was still being used by British Rail as a small, unloved branch line. Gradually the line has been transformed from an industrial line, which never did a great deal except service several collieries, into a scenic country line which provides a major tourist attraction. John Marshall shrewdly points out that the places joined by the line along the valley never had any particular wish to be joined and all had more natural links with other places – there isn't even a road along the valley – so the railway is not serving a geographical function. All it does, apart from act as a living steam museum, is take people sixteen miles from Kidderminster to Bridgnorth and take them back again.

It takes nearly a quarter of a million of them a year, which shows that there is a demand. The idea of an old-fashioned train trip in the country must seem quite appealing if you're living in the West Midlands conurbation. There's something symbolic about the way the line turns away from Kidderminster immediately, goes into a tunnel and re-emerges in the country, as if to say: We're taking you away from all that for the next hour or two. It is very curious, by the way, how the four longer lines in this book, from the West Somerset (twenty two miles) down to the Festiniog (thirteen miles) vary a lot in length but *not* in time – all those lines offer a trip of about sixty or seventy minutes, as if that were the ideal duration of a steam experience. The shorter ones – Keighley, Dart Valley, Bluebell, for example – all opt for half-hour journeys. But the significant statistic lurking in all this is the crucial fact that while there are plenty of shorter lines near urban areas, the Severn Valley Railway as sixteen miles is the *only* longer one in a thickly populated area.

Left: 'Hinton Manor' *draws in to Bewdley station.*

Right: 'The Great Marquess' *outside Bridgnorth loco shed.*

What that means is that they have got the potential customers, the potential volunteers, the potential wealth and the scale of operations to be the best in Britain, *because nobody else has got all those things*. The Keighley and Worth Valley has got the flair and the back-up; the West Somerset has got the countryside and the length; but only the Severn Valley Railway has got the money, the people, the engines and the big track, and you can feel after only a short while there that they have fulfilled most of their potential. They may not be able to boast that they are the longest, oldest or most scenic. All they boast is that they are simply 'Britain's premier steam railway'.

And why not boast that? They have got a wealth of locomotives based at Bridgnorth. They have got as nice a series of stations as most lines, and in Bridgnorth and Bewdley two of the most picturesque small towns in rural England. Their facilities for repairing and rehabilitating engines are second to none. When they got back into Kidderminster, only the SVR would have had the courage to commission the design and building of a brand-new station, modelled on one originally intended for Ross-on-Wye in the last century. In the twenty years since they started operations they have come to be seen as the best established steam line, the one against which others are measured and found wanting. In Michael Draper they have the general manager who has most

Right: *LMS Jubilee class 4-6-0 No. 5690* 'Leander' *on its long climb to Eardington summit.*

Left: *The peaceful Highley station in the early morning light.*

5690
L M S

PASSENGERS ARE
NOT ALLOWED TO CROSS
THE LINE EXCEPT
BY THE BRIDGE
STATION MAS
OFFICE
BOOKIN HALL
KIDDERMINSTER TOWN
5690

made a name for himself with his extrovert personality, his outspoken views on how other lines should be run and how preserved steam should go in the future. That station at Kidderminster got a grant of £60,000 from the English Tourist Board – would any other line have got that?

They are, if you like, the GWR of the preserved steam world. The big lines in the old days all considered themselves great; only the GWR thought it was the greatest, and with some justice. In the Summer of 1989 issue of the *Severn Valley Railway News,* Michael Draper wrote: 'With this spirit, we will maintain our progress, leave our competitors gasping in amazement....' I can't imagine the head of any other line writing such bold, brash stuff.

But the price that the GWR paid for their pre-eminence was that nobody liked them, nobody warmed to their glossy, copper-bottomed confidence. The same is true in a milder sort of way of the SVR, which has ironically taken over part of the GWR set-up. If there was ever a resentment expressed on any line from workers on other railways on my wanderings round Britain last year, it was almost inevitably of the SVR. A bit smug, people said. Too much power. Too much publicity.

All that sort of thing can be put down to jealousy. But there was one more serious idea abroad, and that was that the Severn Valley Railway had over-reached itself at the time of the GWR 150 celebrations in 1985. To celebrate the 150th anniversary of the GWR's founding, British Rail had allowed several big steam-hauled excursions to take place on BR lines. The engines entrusted with this prestigious task had all been provided by the SVR. They all broke down and had to be rescued by BR diesels.

Now, there is nothing particularly shameful in engines breaking down. It happens to BR. It happens to everyone. But three at the same time, and on the same very high-profile occasion.... It started rumours to the effect that the SVR did not look after their engines or other people's engines as well as they might, that pre-eminence had made them a little careless. It led to the illusion that Severn Valley Railway engines on loan to other lines had to be looked at much more carefully. It provoked resentment that after the 1985 débâcle, British Rail made it more difficult and expensive for steam engines to operate on main lines, and people mutter that it was all the SVR's fault.

How true all this is, I do not know. All I can report is that that is what people were saying all over the country, and what interests me here is a railway's image. I cannot imagine that the SVR will lose a moment's sleep over what I say, as they seem to share something else with the old GWR, a genuine indifference to what other people think about them. They still hold the heavyweight championship of the steam world, and it's only carelessness that can beat a true champion.

Enough of this. I have a bouquet to hand out to the Severn Valley Railway now, and it is the award for the

Above: *Many visitors come for the joy of just watching the trains.*

Opposite: *Keen passengers await the arrival of* 'Leander' *at Bewdley station.*

Most Enterprising Licensed Premises on any Steam Railway. Other railways have licences to sell alcohol, but only the SVR has two pubs. One is the King and Castle, a brand new part of the brand new Kidderminster Station but built traditionally rather than with flashing machines and neon lights. The other is the Railwayman's Arms which was part of Bridgnorth Station in old GWR days and in fact never closed down at all during the slow change-over from GWR to SVR; the pints were flowing even when the trains weren't, under a legendary publican called George who was well-known to (a) sell drink after hours, (b) receive stolen goods, depending on which story you hear. It's pleasantly earthy, steamy, unrefurbished and probably much more likely to appeal to the volunteers than the spick and span King and Castle. 1989 was the first year in which Britons were allowed to go into a pub in the afternoon within living memory, and the coming and going of trains between lunch and tea made it fairly busy in the Railwayman's Arms on the afternoons I was in there, which was whenever possible.

'When the season is ended, you breathe a sigh of relief,' says Peter Williamson, catering manager. 'It's lovely and quiet suddenly. Then after about two or three weeks the quiet starts to get very quiet, very silent, and you begin to miss all those people. But at the moment I'm just looking forward to it. Next Thursday, for instance, I have to lay on a Buck's Fizz reception at Kidderminster for a company and its customers, then as soon as they've all got on the train I have to jump in my car, drive the twenty miles to Bridgnorth and get into the pub here, ready for the onslaught as they arrive again. A whole summer of that wears you down.'

He certainly has the experience for this sort of job. He ran pubs in the Birmingham area for a while and before that worked on British Rail dining cars for thirteen years, a useful combination of trains and catering. One of his great delights is trying out new beers in both pubs, so he is deeply offended at being just dropped from *The Good Beer Guide* after thirteen years especially as he can't think of any way in which his pubs have changed, and as he was responsible for the first two beer festivals ever to take place in Shropshire.

'Otherwise no great grumbles, except at being chronically understaffed. All departments are always

Left: *Rearing to go,* 'Leander' *waiting for the signal at Bewdley station.*

Opposite: *Negotiating the approach to Eardington summit.*

2
1

chronically understaffed, whatever they tell you. I have a staff of four to look after two pubs and all the bars on the trains. Except the big bar coach – I've just given that up.' (This is a wonderful coach, empty inside except for a bar running along the *whole* of one side of it. It's my dream to have a party in that coach one day.) 'I seem to have no difficulty in getting licences for special occasions nor have I had any trouble at the King and Castle so far, touch wood.'

Why should he?

'Well, Kidderminster is a rough place, and the station is in a rough section of Kidderminster. Actually, Bridgnorth is rougher than it looks, too.'

It's difficult for an outsider to get any image of Kidderminster at all, as its main feature is a ring road so misleadingly signposted that I have often gone several times round the town trying to find a destination I like the sound of, but it does apparently have a crime level much higher than the average. There were quite a lot of lineside fires in 1989 and some were cases of arson. One volunteer told me that he had been helping the fire brigade put out some fires in a field when he noticed young lads from the nearby housing estate starting more fires, knowing it would probably be blamed on the trains.

Bridgnorth is a much more attractive place at first sight – its position on top of a high red sandstone cliff gives it an appearance of some Italian hill town, and it's a fascinating place to explore. But I have a memory of the place which suddenly comes back to me and suggests that it does have its rougher moments, dating from the time that I was making the *Steam Days* series. I was staying the night at a Bridgnorth hotel with the producer, Neil Cameron, and we'd retired to the bar after dinner to talk about the next day's filming. It suddenly occurred to us how curious it was that although we were quite alone in the bar, there was a tremendous hue and cry going on in the room next door. Cheering, shouting, whistling, shrieks of encouragement.

'Bit of a wild do going on in the function room, sir,' said the young barman, who had an access door at the back. 'All-male gathering. They've had blue comedians and what-not and now they've got a stripper coming on.'

He looked quite cool about it then, but by the third time he'd come round to report, he'd gone pale and was looking a bit shaken.

'She's - er, she's sort of inviting people on stage and getting them to collaborate, as it were. Sir.'

It was then that the hotel manager's wife erupted into the bar. She had just caught sight of what was going on. She was volcanic with rage. She bellowed for her husband. Her husband would have to go up on stage and stop the whole show. As chance would have it, her husband arrived at the very moment from next door, where he'd been watching everything. He was paralytic.

'*There* you are! Darling, the most terrible things are going on next door. You've *got* to stop them now!'

He turned and looked at her as if he'd never seen her before in his life (I got the feeling he was too far gone to recognise her), turned back to the barman and said: 'I want four double scotches for me and my friends', took them on a tray and returned swaying to the fray. The wife burst into tears and fled. Shortly afterwards a middle-aged woman who must have been the star of the show came into the pub to use the phone and ordered a taxi back to Birmingham.

What made all this so extraordinary for Neil and me was that, just like in a Greek play, all the action was reported. We saw nothing. We were two quiet men having a drink in a lonely bar. At the same time we knew exactly what was going on, and could see the repercussions of the whole circus, and if the whole scene had been filmed just as I have described it, some critics would have thought it was brilliant. Whatever else it did, it left me feeling that demure-looking Bridgnorth had its wicked side which might shock anyone who hadn't been to a police force Christmas party or a thrash given by Erich Honecker and his old gang.

The place I liked the look of best was Bewdley, the first

Opposite: *A cheerful Severn Valley volunteer at Hampton Loade station.*

Opposite: 'The Great Marquess' *making its way to Bridgnorth*.

stop out of Kidderminster, which looked as sensational as Bradford-on-Avon, Broadway, Buxton and all those other stunning towns beginning with B, especially as I had never heard of Bewdley before. I refused to discuss Bewdley with anyone on my trips up and down the line, in case it should turn out to have its rough side like Kidderminster or Bridgnorth. I needn't have worried. The people I talked to only wanted to talk about one thing: the railway. The guard who was a schoolteacher ('I think I get more out of being a guard, actually – teaching is an on-going situation with nothing to prove at the end of the day that you've achieved anything, but with a train you can turn round and say: That was on time'). The woman who was the wife of a volunteer working on an engine at Bewdley ('but the teamwork involved has run into the ground a bit. Actually, all the best engines are up the Bridgnorth end, all the good visiting ones, they only get the bog-standard ones down at Kidderminster – it's all to do with politics, of course, I tell you, getting a crane down to Kidderminster is *murder* unless you know the right people'). And Gilbert....

I loved Gilbert. I thought he was great. He thought he was great, too, but that didn't matter. He bounced up to me just when I was feeling a bit rueful after a driver had refused to speak to me. You could tell from the driver's face what he was thinking: 'Oh God, not another expert to tell me that the engine's the wrong livery, or restored wrong, or to ask me what coal I prefer, when all I want is a cup of tea....' He was quite wrong, was Mr Tranter. I wasn't going to ask him anything about engines, which are boring, but about why he wanted to drive one, which is interesting, when this aged man bounced up to me and said:

'Someone told me you were writing a book about this line. Well, let me tell you about this line, and what they should do with it. They should sell all the engines, electrify the whole line from Kidderminster to Bridgnorth and have the whole journey take a minute and a half, including station stops. That's my advice.'

I tried to think of an objection to this revolutionary plan. I thought of one.

'Who'd want to travel on the line then?'

'People with a keen interest in overhead electrification, of course.'

I pulled out my notebook, uncertain whether to write down this unusual view.

'I wouldn't bother,' said Gilbert. 'I'm a nutter, you see.'

He was anything but. He had actually started out life before the Second World War with a desire to rise through the railways, but his father had persuaded him to get out of a career with no prospects (and it was certainly slow work getting promotion in the old days). He had gone into the Royal Tank Corps instead.

'Just in time for the war. Blimey, I was all over the place – Normandy, Africa, Italy, you name it. We had every kind of tank. The Sherman tank was the best we ever had, I liked that, not the Cromwell or any of the others. Well, the Cromwell might have been all right in the desert but it wasn't so hot in the bocage of Normandy.'

He talked about tanks as enthusiasts discuss engines, I noticed.

'We had a great wireless operator out in Egypt, in our tank there. He used to fiddle around with his set and the wires until we could get London on the radio – it was really strange sitting there out in the African desert listening to the home news, Vera Lynn, all that stuff. His name was Michael Bowen. Don't know if you've ever heard of him? He joined the BBC afterwards and went on to become the producer of *Any Questions?* which he did for twenty years or more. My late wife bought me a book of his, all based on the programme, and after she died I made a sort of pilgrimage, I went all the way to his house for him to sign the copy. He wrote in it: "To Claud, in memory of all those rum toddies consumed in tanks in Africa".'

'Claud?' I said.

'I was Claud in the army,' said Gilbert.

'Doing your fair share of drinking and driving,' I said.

3442
L N E R

GREAT WESTERN
2857

'No beathalysers in the desert, son. I think we sometimes had more rum on board than water. Good days, they were.'

It was a strange circle of events, in a way. Alain le Garsmeur, beside doing all the pictures for this book, is also married to the current producer of *Any Questions?*

'After that I eventually joined the police,' said Gilbert, though he didn't say what he was called in the police, 'I was stationed for a long time in Bewdley.'

I ventured to say that I thought Bewdley was a nice place.

'Used to be, used to be. A real community back in those days. In all the time I was there, hardly a hundred new houses were built. Now it's all new estates.... yuppies moving in... it's not the same place at all.'

Doesn't *anybody* round the Severn Valley like *anywhere*? Like all old men, Gilbert was of the opinion that his life would make a good book. As always, I asked him why he didn't write it.

'I have,' was the surprising answer. 'Back in Italy me and a mate sat down to write our war experience, because all the books told so many lies or got it plain wrong. Still got it somewhere. Never got it published, though. But years later someone said to me, Hey, did you know our sergeant had written his own version of the war? Our *Sarge*? I thought. Blimey. So I went out and bought it and read it.'

And how was it?

'He'd got it about right.'

Gilbert was not a well-off old man – he could only afford to volunteer one day if he went off pea-picking at Ombersley the next – so I tried to offer him a fiver as drinking money. I couldn't have done a less tactful thing.

'I have never accepted a bribe in my life!' he said loudly, loudly enough for everyone in the guard's van to stare round curiously. 'In my twenty years on the force I never once took a bribe. Mark you,' he added, relenting slightly, 'I was only ever offered one. Don't mind me, anyway. I'm a nutter.'

I think it was talking to Gilbert that finally unlocked the secret of railway volunteers for me. They may not all be nutters, but they are all odd. Even if they don't say so, they say so indirectly by saying that their wife thinks they're barmy, or, people at work think they're nuts.... It's not being odd that makes them different, though. We're *all* odd. It's having come to terms with their oddness that sets them apart. While the rest of us suffer the delusion of being normal, the railway volunteer is capitalising on his strange urges. He is fulfilling himself. By taking his oddness on board, it is almost as if he has become normal.

It certainly explains why almost all the volunteers I met were quite happy in what they were doing, and furthermore shared in a cameraderie which seemed to go right across the normal class divisions that you get in Britain. The grubby blue overalls or the orange safety gear are great levellers, so you'll find posh undergraduates firing for BR drivers on their week off, or cancer research specialists firing for packers. Railways do have their own divisions (engine shed v. station people, workers v. directors) but there seemed to be almost no enmity between full-time staff and volunteers – the fact that one driver is getting paid and another is not is not nearly so important as the fact that they've both been through the same tests and both love the engines. Nor is there much enmity between lines; a common freemasonry, rather, based on getting stuck in in the same cause. The pub is the natural after hours place for them, and although I can imagine them getting paralytic now and again, I could not visualise them being violent or vicious or turning to drugs. What would be the point? They're hooked on steam already.

This is volunteers I'm talking about, of course, the ones who get their hands dirty. I'm not talking about the enthusiasts with video cameras, notebooks, numbers, histories and solemn faces. I don't know them and I don't entirely trust them. Let me explain why. In the *Independent Magazine* for 2 September 1989 there was a piece by Amanda Mitchison on the Severn Valley Railway. The following week there appeared a

Opposite: *The huge bulk of ex-GWR 2-8-0 No. 2857 waiting in the sidings.*

GREAT WESTERN

Left: *Ex-GWR No. 2857 working its way to Hampton Loade in the evening light.*

letter from N.F. Price of Beckenham, saying among other things:

'In her enthusiasm she has allowed her attention to the facts to be less than scrupulous – a heinous crime in the eyes of railway enthusiasts (the respectable term for grown-up spotters). The Deltic diesel locomotive which she encountered at Kidderminster was far more likely to be a Western, of which two are preserved on the Severn Valley Railway....'

The next week C. Parmenter of Plymouth wrote:-

'Oh dear, oh dear. N.F. Price isn't going to like me very much for pointing out that the locomotive Amanda Mitchison encountered at Kidderminster was very likely a Deltic on loan from the Midland Railway Centre to take part in the Severn Valley's Diesel Gala.... She got the facts right and I'm full of praise for her observation. I only wish there were more journalists who could be accurate when reporting railway facts.'

Well, the price you pay for reporting railway facts, as Amanda Mitchison discovered, is that you bring enthusiasts down on you like a ton of bricks *even when you've got the facts right.* God help you if you get anything wrong. The one fact I gleaned about enthusiasts was that they have the same fervour and Old Testament pedantry as did the New Orleans jazz maniacs amongst whom I spent my youth, and for whom a saxophone was as evil as diesel. The railway newspapers tend to be full of complaints about authenticity, such as criticism that trains in television documentaries very rarely have the right sounds on the soundtrack. Quite justified criticism usually, but I can't help feeling that through having such high standards of accuracy, the enthusiast must make himself quite unhappy most of the time. They certainly don't smile a lot when en masse or out alone, and their expressions on gala weekends do not bring the word 'gala' to mind. If your hear someone roaring with laughter, it'll be a grubby man in an orange safety jacket, not a man behind a camera.

Right: *Enjoying the sun. In between trains at Highley.*

'I think we sometimes get peeved that the public doesn't put its hand in its pocket more,' the man in Bewdley yard with the strong eyes had said to me. 'They don't contribute a lot. They come and look all over this engine and I talk to them patiently, but it's very rarely that I see them put anything in my contributions box here. I wouldn't mind so much if I didn't know how much they spend on expensive videos.'

It was about that time that my hand strayed into my pocket, found the fiver that Gilbert had rejected and somewhat guiltily put it in 7741's Get Well Soon box.

The extraordinary thing is that my final memory of the Severn Valley Line is not one of a volunteer, staff member or enthusiasts. It's of a railwayman who had escaped from railways. If you take the train back from Bridgnorth, and look over a viaduct about a mile along, you will see on the left a mill with a huge water wheel, still working. The sight so intrigued me that I made my way to it by bike and found that it had been restored by Alan George, who had previously worked in railways and on the lorries, but was now producing flour full-time when not showing nosy bicyclists round. I bought some Daniel's Mill flour, admired the gigantic wheel from close to and asked Mr George why he had left trains, gone into mills.

'I married the miller's daughter,' he said.

So there is a cure for railways, after all.

Index

The numbers in **bold** are photographs.